More
Reflections
on The
Meaning
of
Life

More
Reflections
on The
Meaning
of Life

David Friend
and the Editors of

LITTLE, BROWN AND COMPANY
BOSTON TORONTO LONDON

FIRST EDITION

Library of Congress Cataloging-in-Publication information is available.

ISBN 0-316-29409-8

10   9   8   7   6   5   4   3   2   1

BP

Published simultaneously in Canada by Little, Brown & Company (Canada) Limited

PRINTED IN THE UNITED STATES OF AMERICA

This book is dedicated to Shelley Waln,
for her passion, vision, persistence and friendship,
and to the memory of Martin Sumner.

EDITOR David Friend
DESIGNERS Tom Bentkowski, Mimi Park
PICTURE EDITOR Peggy S. Allen
ASSISTANT EDITOR Henry Sidel
COPY CHIEF Nikki Amdur
CORRESPONDENTS *Africa, Central America*
David Ewing Duncan
Asia
Karen Emmons
Eastern Europe
Tala Skari
North America
Jack Hayes
South America
Linda Gomez
REPORTERS Amy Paulsen
Jennifer Reek
Ariel Zeitlin
BUREAU STAFFS *Ankara*
Mehmet Ali Kislali
Beijing
Mia Turner
Bonn
Kanta Stanchina, Leny Heinen
Cairo
Amany Radwan
Jerusalem
Marlin Levin, Joshua R. Simon
London
Liz Corcoran, Liz Nickson,
Gail Ridgwell
Los Angeles
Jim Calio, Fritz Yuvancic
Moscow
Constance Richards
Nairobi
Joseph Ngala
New Delhi
Anita Pratap
Paris
Hélène Veret
Rome
Mimi Murphy
Sydney
Maggy Sterner
Tokyo
S. Chang
NEWS BUREAU CHIEF Bonnie J. Smith
NEWS DESK Claudia Gorelick, Alexander Smith
COPY DESK Barbara Mead, Melissa Pierson
DESIGN ASSISTANTS Carolyn Carpenter, Tom Vincent
INSPIRATION Molly and Sam Friend,
Nancy Rose Paulsen

Acknowledgments

LIFE managing editor and publisher Jim Gaines has been instrumental in assuring that this book see the light of day.

Others who have helped make this volume possible include: Matthew Antezzo, Joe Aprea, Miles Barth, Janie Joseland Bennett, Jocelyne Benzakin, Barry Bishin, Cynthia Borg, Patti Boustany, Neil Burgess, Barbara Baker Burrows, Ben Chapnick, Howard Chapnick, Jennifer Coley, Naomi Cutner, Leona Dodsworth, Cindy Dopkin, Azurea Lee Dudley, Christina Eckerson, Ruth Eichhorn, Linda Ferrer, Mike Gentry, Alice Rose George, June Goldberg, Kate Grant, Mark Greenberg, Charles Hirshberg, David Hollander, Carla Howarth, Jim Hubbard, Regina Joseph, Carol Kismaric, Hanns Kohl, Eliane Laffont, Douglas Lenat, Laleli Lopez, Peter Meyer, Valery Moore, Larry Nesbitt, Jean-Jacques Naudet, Diane Nilsen, Alex Nolan, Frank Perich, Virginia Perrin, William Phillips, Françoise Piffard, Robert Pledge, David Portnoy, Helgard Repp-Gulow, Beth Richardson, Albert Rufino, Pat Ryan (who started it all), Barbara Sadick, Marie Schumann, Mary Shea, Jeffrey Smith, Dieter Steiner, Rick Sullo, Leslie Tonkonow, David Van Biema and Diane Wright.

Among those who have helped develop, support or encourage projects centered around the Meaning of Life theme are:

Kim Adams, Lori Almquist, Jay Amestoy, Rick Balsiger, Katy Barr, Maggie Barrett, Laura Bennett, Robin Bierstedt, Bryan Birch, Dan Brewster, Regis Boff, Kate Bonniwell, Bonny Botts, Teymour Boutros-Ghali, Reg Brack, Kathleen Burrows, Mary Carragher, Michael Chadsey, Phil Crihfield, Mary Anne Christy, Jools Clarke, Beth Cole, Ed Cole, Harry Cukurs, Linda Colleran, Tim Conley, Barbara Czerniel, Robert Daly, Ray Damiano, Gedeon de Margitay, Steve Deschenes, Barbara Dillon, Mark Dodge, Sandy Drayton, Kathleen Drohan, Clint Ehlers, Fred Ehlers, Don Elliman, Carole Fabale, Rich Fairfield, Deborah Feyerick, Laury Frieber, Andrew Freedman, Jerry Fronczak, Spencer Geissinger, Jeffrey Getis, Paula Glatzer, David Goldberg, Murray Goldwaser, Lesley Gould, Joel Griffiths, Dana Gruskin, Bill Hagelstein, Duke Hale, Terri Hamman, Bob Hammond, Priscilla Hanrihan, Dick Heinemann, Jim Helberg, Lynn Hillenburg, Mark Hintsa, Lee Holden, Donn Hoyer, Laura Hynes, Chuck Jennes, Cory Johnson, Wendy Johnson, Harry Johnston, Bob Jones, Quincy Jones, Bruce Judson, Kensuki Kato, Steve Kerho, Ed Kjaer, Larry Kopald, Angie Kunz, Bill Kupper, Christina Landon, Norman Lear, Len Lieberman, Liz Leow, Gerald Levin, Leah Lindberg, Charlotte Loontiens, Steve MacDonald, Rob Mahalak, Joel Maliniak, Marilee Marshall, Preston Marshall, Sandy Marshall, Jan Mason, George McCabe, Mike McClelland, Jason McManus, Chris Meigher, Barry Meyer, Bob Miller, Jim Murry, Joseph Natalie, Roger Neal, Gary Necessary, Nick Nicholas, Brian Norwood, Gene Otaki, Tom Ott, Dave Palsmento, Jim Paratore, Laura Parker, Dave Parmenter, Rod Paul, Linda Pevac, Nancy Phillips, Barbara Pierce, Jack Pitney, Andrea Porfilio, Gavin Powers, Mark Pylypczuk, Joe Quinlan, Rick Raymond, Amy Rea, Sandy Reisenbach, Aviva Rahmani, Gil Rogin, Liz Rosenberg, Bruce Rosenbloom, Gregory Ross, Steve Ross, Jeff Sagansky, David Salzman, Marianne Sauvage, Elayne Sawaya, Val Scansaroli, Aaron Schindler, George Schlatter, Maria Schlatter, Steve Seabolt, Margaret Sedgwick, Terry Semel, John Sheridan, Elaine Shock, Ann Jacobson Shure, Gianna Sibella, Greg Sieck, Ursula Smith, Tom Somerset, Kazuo Sonoguchi, Norma Staikos, Debra Stanek, Suzzanne Stangel, Ann Stanley, Joncea Stemnock, Mark St. Germain, Dick Stolley, Ricki Tarlow, Takeshi Tatsuta, Yoshinori Taura, Celsa Terry, Jeff Theisen, Lisa Thomas, Sharon Thomas, Jan Thompson, Tony Timov, Lindsay Valk, Eleanor Van Bellingham, John Varty, Clark Vitulli, Steve Warner, Dave Weber, Gretchen Wessels, Chris Whelan, Yukio Yabe, Steve Ybarra, Jeff Young, Ann Zacarian and Felix Zepeda.

Catherine Henriette
HIGH PRIEST IN TRAINING, SAMYE, TIBET

Introduction

Everything is too rushy," says Emran Majid, a taxi driver from Brunei. Joe Flying Bye, a South Dakota medicine man, agrees: "You have to relax in this hurry life. Rest while you're thinking. This will give you time to see straight. Then you will get the idea what life is."

This book asks readers to slow down, to take time to get a different perspective so that a sense of the bigger picture can emerge.

The big picture, of course, is what LIFE magazine has always been about: outsize photographs that capture the human condition, life-affirming stories that reveal deeper truths connecting us all. And this volume is about the biggest picture of all. Produced by the editors of LIFE, *More Reflections on the Meaning of Life* uses powerful photos and poignant, personal essays to bring the purpose (or absurdity) of existence into sharper focus.

More Reflections is the sequel to LIFE magazine's celebrated collection *The Meaning of Life*, which addresses the ultimate issue of this or any age. Expanding the scope of the first book (printed in black and white), *More Reflections* juxtaposes vivid color images by 137 of the world's premier photographers with passionate and provocative observations from an international roster of 225 contributors, both well known and unknown. The result is a global mosaic of impressions on why we exist—362 "answers" from Mario Cuomo and Michael Jackson, Corazon Aquino and Sinéad O'Connor, Benazir Bhutto and Eduard Shevardnadze, Garrison Keillor and Yogi Berra, a Balinese dancer and an Incan priest. Each of the pictures on these pages—depicting scenes in 36 countries and on the moon—conveys a sense of the purpose of existence. Each of the written statements—from men and women (and even one computer) in 53 nations—is a response to one of two questions: "What is the meaning of life?" or "Why are we here?"

How does a team of journalists cover the ultimate story? Throughout one long summer I dispatched some of LIFE's best correspondents to the ends of the earth. Their assignment: to comb the globe for sages-in-the-street, to probe and prod for anecdote and wisdom, to be one part Kurault and two parts Kerouac.

To that end, Linda Gomez chewed coca leaves with witches in Bolivia for two and half days. In the Philippines, Karen Emmons commiserated with a dentist clad in a pith helmet as the pair fled the fury of an erupting volcano. In Panama, David Ewing Duncan hacked through jungle underbrush to find willing subjects near a virgin rain forest. In Hungary, Tala Skari conducted her first interview in the nude—conversing with a bathhouse masseuse. Closer to home, Jack Hayes left skid marks in 16 states in his search for the truth, developing calluses on his driving hands. And all the while Henry Sidel and I, based in Manhattan, the capital of the "hurry life," used fax and phone to coax profundity from statesmen, celebrities and the otherwise less obscure.

Photographers were easier to locate; Peggy Allen and I were deluged with submissions, many containing children scampering or water splashing. Some photographers sent stacks of images, covering the widest thematic range imaginable. Others, like Henri Cartier-Bresson, provided a single, perfect frame (his choice, evocative of Beckett, showed a couple in hesitant embrace—in a graveyard). As a rule, however, a selection of favorite pictures was shipped in by photographers or their agencies, accompanied by what amounted to a good-natured shrug: *You* choose one, please.

More Reflections on the Meaning of Life, masterfully designed by Tom Bentkowski and Mimi Park, tries to offer an eclectic mix of truth and myth, and all the magic in between. As the millennium nears its close, as the world of nations swells to sample democracy firsthand, as faith has come to replace fear in many lands, as the human family becomes acutely aware of the fragility of the planet, there has never been a time better suited for slowing down the pace of things—and for savoring the kind of messages presented here.

—*David Friend*

Jay Ullal
MAUNI BABA OF THE
SADHU-GURU CULT, INDIA

(Overleaf)
Joe McNally
CHRISSY NELON SHARES A HUG

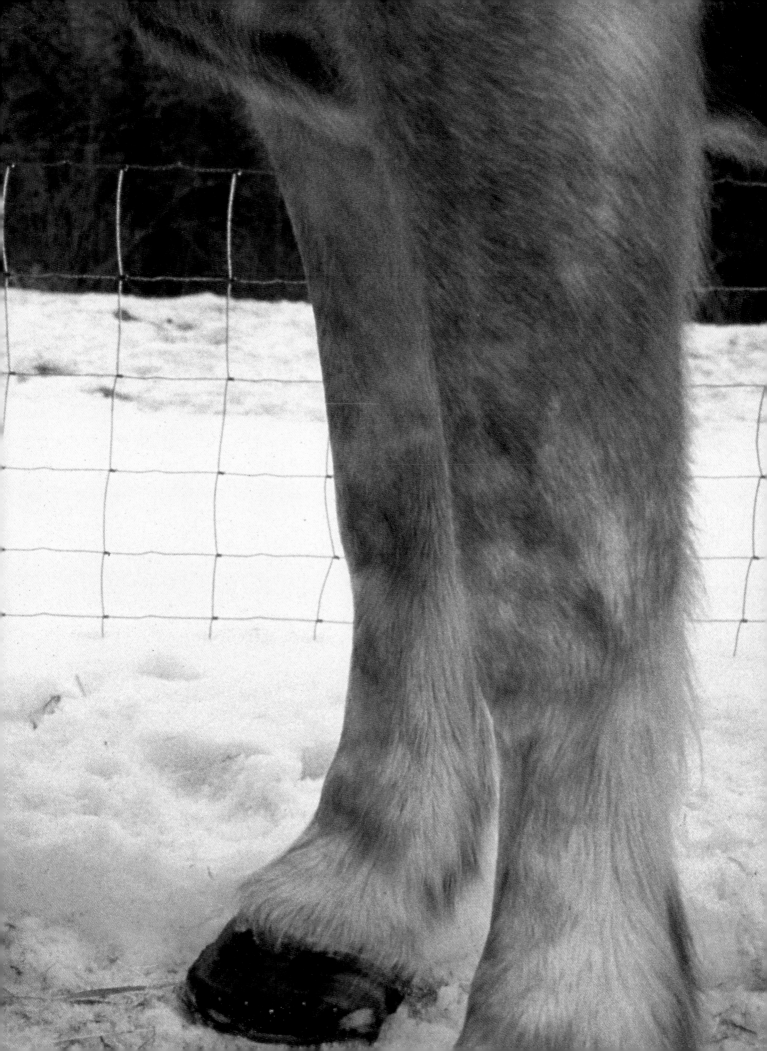

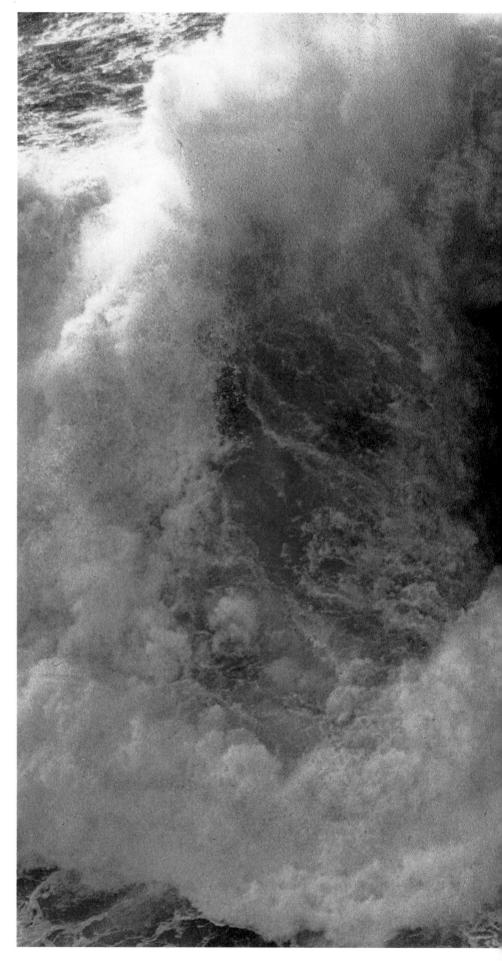

A man said to the universe:
"Sir, I exist!"
"However," replied the universe,
"The fact has not created in me
A sense of obligation."

While my grade school friends were reading Kipling, I took pleasure in poems similar to the one by Stephen Crane cited here. Somehow, as a child, I had intimations of what I came to learn as an adult: The sunsets don't give a damn. They were as heartbreaking in their beauty illuminating the bleached skulls on the killing fields of Cambodia as they were reddening the sails of Newport yachts. The stars came out just as brilliantly on the ruins of a bombed church in Birmingham, Alabama, as they did for night skiers on the pristine mountaintops of Denver, Colorado.

The universe is a blank slate. And I believe there is no meaning to life. There are only valiant efforts to ward off the truth of an intrinsic void—individually and collectively—by coining a vocabulary of constructive behavior within the small unit of self, on toward the greater unit of a society. And at any given moment, on any point of this planet, that vocabulary is in flux and in danger of becoming babble. Suicide evidences an individual losing the language of life and witnessing this internal void; genocide and world wars evidence a collective loss of such language. Will there come a time when we forget how to speak altogether? The jury is still out.

Gloria Naylor,

American novelist and essayist, is the author of *The Women of Brewster Place*

Jean Guichard
LIGHTHOUSE KEEPER, BRITTANY COAST

A musician traveling in a hot, dry country came upon a procession in a small village. Dancing through the dusty streets were men, women and children in robes of orange and purple silk, with yellow powder on their faces. In the middle of the parade, borne aloft on a litter covered with flowers, were the bronze statues of two lions. It was the day of the annual Feast of the Temple Guardians.

At noon the celebrants entered the temple and closed the heavy wood doors behind them, leaving the musician to wander the deserted streets. Overwhelmed by sunlight, he stepped into a shaded courtyard. Fountain-stirred water tumbled from terrace to terrace into pools arranged geometrically among fruit trees. In a room facing the garden he found a piano and notebooks filled with music paper. And in this cool marble-walled room, to the accompaniment of birds outside a grilled window, he sat down and composed for the first time in years. Hours of effortless composition were followed by the sound of an explosion coming from the street. His trance interrupted, the musician paused to take stock of what he had written—one long symphonic work he had titled, at the outset, *The Song of God*.

Carrying his achievement in the many notebooks under his arm, he stepped out into the street. Night had fallen. The streets had been watered down. And children, with the faint traces of yellow powder on their faces, were throwing firecrackers against the sides of the houses.

Janet Hamill
is an American poet

Sumio Uchiyama
MAHARAJA'S WEDDING, INDIA

Christopher Morris
VETERANS DAY AT VIETNAM
VETERANS MEMORIAL WALL

Brad Burt

God existed but no one knew he did, so he created people so at least one person would know.

I am Hindu; I am Balinese. I believe that the best life is when you can understand it's more important what you have inside than outside. You need to balance food for the body with food for the spirit. In Bali we have strong religion, culture, custom. This is our system for spirit food. We have special musical instruments, dances, temples with carvings. I paint Balinese stories about what God means, what life means. Culture is my feeling. What we feel on the inside, people want to see on the outside. To do this we have a system called *tatwamasi*. I'm you, you're me. Example: I talk to someone. When we have a good talk, he gets a good feeling. He has a good feeling, I get reflection of that good feeling.

This is all I own: two shirts, three sarongs, two pairs of shoes. That's my life and that makes me happy. One we wash, one we use. That means we're harmonious. Balinese have something called *duabeneda*. Two different things are always one. You can't see the good without the bad, hot without cold. To be harmonious with God you must always think: out-in, in-out. This is the meaning of life: people to people, people to God, people to nature. God made our spirit, feeling and power. All three things together bring harmonious harmony.

I Dewa Nyoman Batuan
is a painter who lives in Ubud, Bali

Once upon a time, long, long ago, there were some people who had such incredibly advanced technology they were able to build time machines and transporter booths in which they could move freely through space. Eventually, they were able to bilocate themselves—to copy themselves in time and space. After they got the technology working, they had quite a thrill—for the first few seconds. Then a deep boredom set in because they were no longer surprised by anything. They had been everywhere. They had seen the future.

So they decided to play another game. They said to themselves: "We're going to forget our technology, and we're going to plunk ourselves down in caves and live the primitive life. Then we will grow old and have children who relearn the technology." In fact, before the second game, they had already seen this scenario with the help of their technology, but they decided that in order to have genuine experiences, they would have to exist in a state that allowed for an element of surprise.

Then we descended. And now we're on our way back to remembering.

This myth expresses the fundamental stagnation of omniscience, which, in many traditions, has been described as the reason why the universe came into being. Life is based on limitation and compromise. The fact that we forget the meaning of life is the meaning of life. Being in a state of partial awareness allows experience and life to progress. God, as an omniscient being, is not an "experiencing being" because his or her experience is not new.

If You were going to start a universe, what would Your options be? You could choose to remain totally stagnant, but that wouldn't amount to a true universe. You'd need entities that experience it, entities that are fragile and temporary and not omniscient. That's who we are and why we're here.

Jaron Lanier,
scientist, visionary and entrepreneur, is one of the pioneers of virtual reality, a computer-simulated three-dimensional world

We humans are here because God wanted to behold God. He created us in His image and gave us free will to behave one way or another, to choose between doing the job of reflecting Him and doing what looks more exciting.

I'm here to know myself. Since I can't achieve this without understanding God's ideas about why we're here, I've made it my goal to find out what Jesus was really "on" about, and live accordingly. One lesson I've learned from Him is that when you know something's true and something else is a lie, you have to choose between the two and be prepared to die for that choice.

Jesus showed us, in His crucifixion, that once you know the truth and can see it all around you, nothing can kill you. If you stick to what you know is true, there is no human death. Everything He did, we can do too. A lot of people have gone through the same thing Jesus did, but Jesus is the most famous. The purpose of life is to find the truth and make it come into everything you do, from one end of the day to the other. You may be a rock star and you may work in Woolworth's, but you have to apply the truth to all of your pursuits.

To know yourself, you've got to let go of everything you've clung to. You have to make a leap of faith and say, "I'm not going to lie to myself anymore." It's the scariest thing in the whole world to release these self-perceptions, but, if you trust in God, you'll be all right.

Sinéad O'Connor
is an Irish-born singer and songwriter

Georgi Pinkhassov
SELF-PORTRAIT, BAKOU, U.S.S.R.

Animals will fight to the death to try to survive. Even if it's a rattlesnake swallowing a gopher. The gopher tries to get away, but after the snake gets ahold of him, he's going down. That's the way it is with a human too. I saw animals fight, I saw people fight when the odds were against them. They know they're going to get whipped, but they'll fight to the death to try to stay alive. It isn't any particular thing we're living for, just the instinct to stay alive. But I'm no authority.

Robert Wilkoske,

salvage professional, owns a Cheyenne, Wyoming, wrecking company

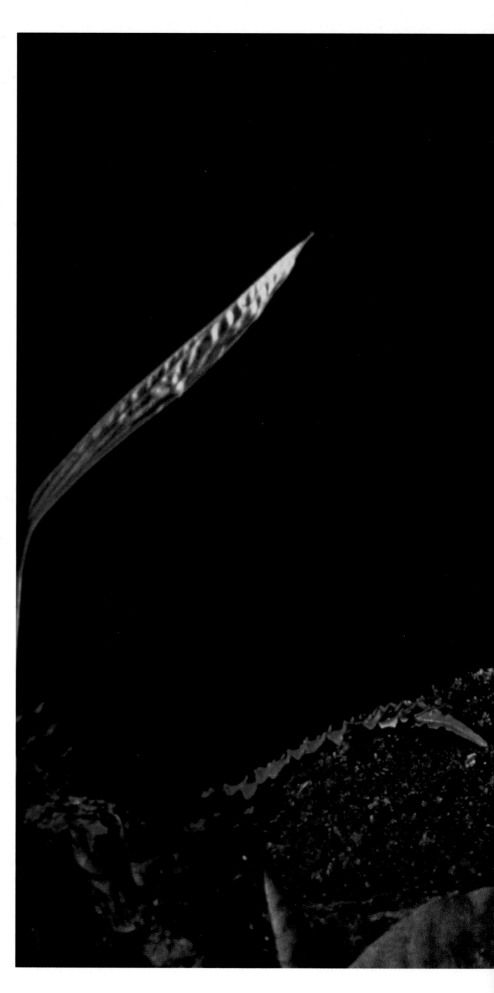

Merlin D. Tuttle
FROG-EATING BAT

I am five or six years old. It is early morning. I am sitting outside Mother's house, perched on the logs that support her granary. The morning is clear, cool; my black skin is soaking in the sun's early warmth. I fall into a reverie. "Here I am sitting by Mother's granary," I muse. "How has this come about? How did I, Marwa, come to be a human being? How is it that I sit here feeling the warmth of the morning sun?"

The answer comes as an epiphany. If God would have not been, then I, Marwa, would not have been. God is both the purpose (the why) and manner (the how) of my existence.

For me, as a child growing up in a small village, family life was important. But our village also had members on the other side of the grave. We thought of these ancestors as the living dead. We even thought of the unborn as villagers, and it was important to bear children, thus releasing the unborn into the living part of the village family. As such, I heard little mention of an active God. In the oral tradition of the Luo people, stories describe a distant God who had concerned himself, at one time, with the daily affairs of village life, a God who later moved away for some reason, leaving people to fend for themselves. The Luo name for God, *Nyasay Nyakalaga,* means God the creator, the originator, the source. If a woman became pregnant, if someone had escaped from a crocodile or a snake, people would say, *Nyasay osekonyi* (God has helped you).

But that morning, as I sat by Mother's granary, it came to me that God, in fact, was my reason for being, that beyond village activity and relationships, there was one power in whom all things and all events had their beginning and purpose, *Nyasay Nyakalaga.*

Several years later two Christian evangelists, both Luo men, passed through. I was herding goats with several small boys on the savanna. The men, walking along the footpath, called us to come to the shade of a tree. These were the first Christians I had ever seen. I didn't think of them as men of God. These two men sang the most beautiful song for us. The tune was strange and ethereal, a melody drawing us out of the dusty savanna, lifting us beyond our circle of knowledge and experience. The words were in Luo, speaking of God; the music was like the wind whispering in the trees.

Next they read from a book that said that God loves people and that he sent his Son to the world so that any person could have eternal life. Anyone who welcomed God's Son into the circle of his life would be accepted by God; those who made themselves enemies of God's Son would be destroyed in everlasting fire. This was a new kind of life and death they were talking about—a reality beyond the circle of the village and its concern with the ancestors.

In a few weeks they came again, and their message was the same. They spent the night in Father's village sleeping in the youth house. The next morning they went on their way.

Marwa Kisare
is the first Mennonite bishop of the Luo tribe of Tanzania

Life is that stuff that binds together everything in all categories, that ties the unborn to the born, the living to the dead, the things you remember to the things you will see in the future. It's also that thing that ties what you are seeing to what you are feeling about it.

I had an experience once. I was going to a wedding in Ojinaga, Mexico. It turned out I got on the wrong bus. Instead of going to Ojinaga, it went to Marfa, so I had to get off in Marfa, which is in the mountains. From five in the afternoon, all night, up and down through the hills, I walked toward Ojinaga, 64 miles away.

In the middle of the night I was out there in the sierra, which was very desolate, very isolated. And as I was walking, these birds began to gather in front of me— all sorts of birds. As I approached them, they would make all this racket and then move back. Then they'd sort of wait for me. I'd walk closer, and they'd make all this noise and move back. All night they did this. Silence . . . approach . . . fly off again. I started observing details, identifying particular birds even though it was quite dark. I would get close enough to see them eye to eye. It was as if they perceived me, giving me certain looks.

Now my grandmother and uncles talked about all these things they'd see in the sierra. My people have the belief that you will meet people in the desert who are not really in existence. Anyway, as I was dealing with the birds, I was thinking: "Why should I have any fear out here? My family has been living here for generations." All the people who passed onto the dead world would be here, and they would know that I am Monica's son and Petra's grandson and Eduvijes's great-grandson. And if there is any spirit out there—this element of life—that could have any kind of influence over me, it would be my kin, people who would have an interest in advancing my existence because it would protect and prolong theirs.

That night I strongly felt this element. I was communicating with these birds somehow. I don't think the birds were directed in any way or that they were actually my relatives. I think this element I'm calling life is too comprehensive to be so directed or so specific. But there I was, communing with it. It made me feel very secure. I sensed that I was walking through that sierra in balance, not in any way disturbing life out there such that it would reject me, that a snake would bite me or a coyote would try to attack me. I didn't see anything the entire night that frightened me. I walked until about 10 o'clock the next morning, and an uncle of mine happened to drive by and pick me up.

That night I felt tapped into what life really was, from what I saw to what I felt, from what I could see and what I could not. And I thought, "This does not die. This does not go away. This is not a small thing. It is a very big thing, and it is not something that I can lose. I may ignore it or take it for granted, but I will not lose it." I felt that if I should die everything would have been O.K. because I felt there was no death and no beginning or end and, therefore, nothing about myself that I needed to protect.

Oscar Rodriguez
is the city manager of Eagle Pass, Texas

When I was 19, I was raped. They held a gun to my head. They played Russian roulette, three empty chambers, three full. They pulled the trigger a couple of times. That experience was very formative. Most people don't look down the barrel of mortality until later in life. In the course of the experience, something flipped over and I went beyond fear. Anyone who comes very, very close to losing his life—then has it given back—literally has a new lease on life, a lease written on different terms than the old. Some say such people live out their lives to justify the saving of it.

After that, I quit wasting time. I cut out inessentials. There were no more projects sitting around in the drawer waiting for me to get to them someday. There was no more not telling people things I felt, not expressing the love I felt.

Some people don't need to have a telegram wrapped around a brick and flung through their window to get their attention. Either there's meaning to life or there's not. You can't really add meaning. Either you have a sense of what you're here for and you make things point to it or you don't.

Crescent Dragonwagon
is a children's book author, innkeeper and chef from Eureka Springs, Arkansas

Poppa taught me a lot about life, especially its hard times. I remembered one of his lessons one night when I was ready to quit a political campaign I was losing, and wrote about it in my diary:

Tired, feeling the many months of struggle, I went up to the den to make some notes. I was looking for a pencil, rummaging through papers in the back of my desk drawer, where things accumulate for years, when I turned up one of Poppa's old business cards, the ones we made up for him, that he was so proud of: *Andrea Cuomo, Italian-American Groceries—Fine Imported Products*. Poppa never had occasion to give anyone a calling card, but he loved having them.

I couldn't help wondering what Poppa would have said if I told him I was tired or—God forbid—discouraged. Then I thought about how he dealt with hard circumstances. A thousand pictures flashed through my mind, but one scene came sharply into view.

We had just moved to Holliswood, New York, from our apartment behind the store. We had our own house for the first time; it had some land around it, even trees. One, in particular, was a great blue spruce that must have been 40 feet tall.

Less than a week after we moved in, there was a terrible storm. We came home from the store that night to find the spruce pulled almost totally from the ground and flung forward, its mighty nose bent in the asphalt of the street. My brother Frankie and I could climb poles all day; we were great at fire escapes; we could scale fences with barbed wire—but we knew nothing about trees. When we saw our spruce, defeated, its cheek on the canvas, our hearts sank. But not Poppa's.

Maybe he was five feet six if his heels were not worn. Maybe he weighed 155 pounds if he had a good meal. Maybe he could see a block away if his glasses were clean. But he was stronger than Frankie and me and Marie and Mamma all together.

We stood in the street looking down at the tree. The rain was falling. Then he announced, "O.K., we gonna push 'im up!" "What are you talking about, Poppa? The roots are out of the ground!" "Shut up, we gonna push 'im up, he's gonna grow again." We didn't know what to say to him. You couldn't say no to him. So we followed him into the house and we got what rope there was and we tied the rope around the tip of the tree that lay in the asphalt, and he stood up by the house,

with me pulling on the rope and Frankie in the street in the rain, helping to push up the great blue spruce. In no time at all, we had it standing up straight again!

With the rain still falling, Poppa dug away at the place where the roots were, making a muddy hole wider and wider as the tree sank lower and lower toward security. Then we shoveled mud over the roots and moved boulders to the base to keep the tree in place. Poppa drove stakes in the ground, tied rope from the trunk to the stakes, and maybe two hours later looked at the spruce, the crippled spruce made straight by ropes, and said, "Don't worry, he's gonna grow again. . . ."

I looked at the card and wanted to cry. If you were to drive past that house today, you would see the great, straight blue spruce, maybe 65 feet tall, pointing straight up to the heavens, pretending it never had its nose in the asphalt.

I put Poppa's card back in the drawer, closed it with a vengeance. I couldn't wait to get back into the campaign.

Mario Cuomo
is the governor of New York

(Overleaf)
Marco A. Cruz
PASSION PLAY, IXTAPALAPA, MEXICO

The meaning of life lies in the oneness of all creation, which combines supreme diversity with supreme interdependence.

It is only now that people are learning that whatever we do as individuals carries a consequence in society and whatever societies do affects the whole world. We can no longer allow ourselves to pursue ends that merely further immediate gain. We have depleted the planet's resources, its wealth of flora and fauna. We have reduced populations to famine and sickness. We have exploited children in the workplace without a further thought of the consequences. Today, these consequences have caught up with us and we are indeed threatened with the biblical Four Horsemen of the Apocalypse.

There may still be time to think of the welfare of our children. We are one with creation in time and space. We cannot hope for a future without understanding our past. We cannot hope for health without understanding the sources of sickness. We cannot hope for joy unless we understand inevitable pain. We bear a great responsibility, as much to ourselves as we do to everything that lives on air and water.

Yehudi Menuhin,
American violinist, made his debut
with the San Francisco Orchestra at age seven

Leonard Hayflick
SENESCENT HUMAN CELLS

J ust as different streams of color mix to form white light, so deeds done in one's various past lives form the blueprint for the next life. It is my karma that has made me feel that attaining God is the most important thing. The meaning of life is to attain God.

Life is an ocean. I am somewhere on the high seas of life. It's difficult to explain where I am because there are no signposts. But I am still searching for God. Once man attains his goal, he will achieve spiritual bliss. Just as a mute cannot express taste, so we cannot describe what spiritual bliss is all about.

Guru Bhagwandasacharya

is a 90-year-old high priest in Vrindaban, India, the birthplace of the Hindu god Krishna

Dennis Kunkel
MAGNIFIED EPINEPHRINE
AND PYROGALLIC ACID CRYSTALS

The meaning of life is contained in every single expression of life. It is present in the infinity of forms and phenomena that exist in all of creation. Life blooms into flowers, love songs, music, and explodes into stars, nebulae and galaxies.

We exist in a living, pulsating, dancing universe, and we are a privileged species because the creative force of all life is most alive in our souls.

Each of us arrives on this planet with a purpose. To fulfill that purpose is to ignite the spark of divinity in us and give meaning to our lives.

Michael Jackson,
whose album *Thriller* is the top-selling recording in history, is the world's best-known musical performer

Brian Lanker
TAIJIQUAN: DANCE OF THE FALSE TOMBS

Dion Johnson
WATER FIGHT

Martine Franck

Victoria Ginn
Forest Spirits, Makira,
Solomon Islands

JK: I know the sounds of the birds. Certain sounds mean something bad will happen. If we're at the farm and hear the sound, we go back home. Also, if we have bad dream—if we dream of snakes or teeth—we don't go out.

KP: We live by our dreams. If I have a good dream, for sure something good will happen. If I have bad dream and don't bother about it, when harvesting pepper I don't get much from the harvest or I get a high fever. I am pagan. I believe in the spirits. My earrings show maturity. These tattoos are for bravery and give us memory of travels we've made. The ones on my front shoulders are cucumbers. There's one of an insect, a leech, a crab. A person who doesn't have them should be scared of me. Headhunters have them on the fingers—that's the most brave tattoo. I never head-hunted because I was small during that time. The white raja stopped it. Some customs, like the tattoo, now are no more. When we go hunting and fishing, we used to wear warrior clothes. Now we wear simple clothes because it's modern and easy. Everybody wants to be modern, and I want to be modern.

JK: Life in the longhouse is different from life in the town. We must stay together, obey the chief. We have strict rules to help people square with each other. Every race has its own ceremonies and customs. It would be bad if we lost our tradition. We can't forget it. We must keep it and teach it and carry it on. This may be the most important thing we do with our lives. Our purpose is also to see the world, to see development. We don't leave the life in the forest, but we must follow the new life. My grandfather had no chair, but now I have chair.

KP: My purpose is to be alive in this world and do things like build house and find something to eat. What I have makes me happy. Rice is our life. Without rice, we don't survive.

Jeffry Keroh,
assistant chief of the Mejong longhouse, and
Kudang Ak Panyu,
farmer, are Iban tribesmen in Sarawak, Borneo

Imagine yourself as someone who lived 100,000 years ago in the forests of the African plateau, someone who lived by hunting and gathering and whose speech was only partially developed. You might not have had a word for life, yet your survival would have depended crucially on an instantaneous recognition of living things. As you traveled through the forest you would have always been on guard; for behind that tree ahead or in that clump of rocks to the left might lurk a plump wild boar, your mate or a tiger. Life for you was something edible, lovable or lethal. All of these needed immediate recognition, not the leisurely processes of conscious reasoning. So important for survival was the ability to speedily distinguish living animals from dead rocks, or verdant background, that it must have become an instinct, part of the fast but unconscious machine-language of the mind.

Only in recent times have we enjoyed the luxury of wondering consciously about the meaning of life in the high-level languages of speech and writing. We should not be surprised that it, like intelligence, is difficult to define. Some dictionaries do not even try, listing life as something "not dead." And the dictionary of biology does not list it at all. If pushed, a biologist will say life is something that reproduces and corrects the errors of reproduction by natural selection. Hardly a satisfactory definition, for it rules out most grandmothers, Lombardy poplar trees, ecosystems and Gaia.

James Lovelock,
British scientist and inventor, is the creator of the Gaia theory, which holds that the planet Earth is a living entity

As children we learned the meaning of life from the elders of the village as we sat in the circle of the fire. My grandmother liked to tell the story of two men. One was blind and one could not walk. They were working together, you see. The blind man carried the crippled man on his back. One had the feet; the other had the eyes. One day, they met a lion. The blind man just threw the crippled man away and ran. The crippled one was killed by the lion because he couldn't run; the blind one because he couldn't see.

As people, you must live together, especially in an unhappy situation. This is the main purpose of the African in traditional life: to live with his community, to protect others. There are lions everywhere, you know.

It is the will of God that I was born chief. This is my purpose. Our people believe the chief is created by God as the link to our ancestors. There must be somebody at the lead to say: "Thou shall not steal. Thou shall not kill." Man is a clever animal and must be watched. There must be somebody who directs the people to make their lives purposeful. I do not favor anyone. Until I die, this is what I promise my gods, through my ancestors.

Chief Linchwe II,
head of the Bakgatla tribe, is one of the founders of Botswana

Life is a flower, spirit is the bloom.
Everyone knows spirits exist even though we can't see them. Each of us has a spirit that never dies; it simply moves to another world, serving as a bridge between this world and another. When we die our spirit walks for eight days and nights. Three days after my father's death in 1979, his spirit entered our home. We didn't see it, but we became dizzy and were frightened even though spirits can do no harm. Dogs can see spirits better than any other animal. Birds can hear spirits. When they whistle at night, someone will soon die.

They say the Inca spirits still exist. There is a town, Yuncapata, way off in the mountains, from which it takes the villagers a couple of days to walk to Cuzco. I buy the potatoes villagers bring, and they tell me people have seen the Incas. They only see them from a distance, because when they come closer, the Incas disappear. The villagers don't try to approach them anymore; by keeping at a distance, they can see the Incas all day.

Spirits show us life is much more than what we can see. After this world there is the other world. I wonder, does the other world have another world as well?

Arturo Leguía
is a craftsman and artisan living in Cuzco, Peru

Nature brought me into this world to play the music, to be a man who makes people feel good. If you develop your natural gift, there's no better satisfaction in life, no better purpose. I play the mambo, waltzes, polkas, Latin music—everything. The people on the beach here, they may not applaud anymore, but they tell me, "Angelo, that's very good." The best satisfaction for me is when I play and the people are dancing and squealing. I just get out of this world.

I am a satisfied person. The basic key to having a happy life is to live until you *know* you're satisfied. What am I going to do with a few million dollars? If I'd try to use it, I'd get sick. I have grandchildren, a wife of 56 years. I eat pork, yucca, rice, and I'm happy.

"Manisero" is a very old Cuban song from the 1930s about a peanut vendor. He's begging people to buy his peanuts, very nicely roasted and salted. His philosophy is my philosophy: Buy my peanuts, they are nice, and you are going to enjoy, and the more you eat, the more you'll dance and the more fun you'll have.

Here, I'll play it for you:

In Cuba, each merry maid
wakes up with this serenade:
Pea-nuts!
They're nice and hot.
Pea-nuts!
I sell a lot.
If you haven't got bananas,
don't be blue,
Pea-nuts in a little bag
are calling you.*

Angelo Jaspe,
former pianist for Pinkie Arias and His Panamanian All-Stars, plays organ at a beachside cabana in San Carlos, Panama

Mauro Galligani
BISTRO SERENADE, SCARDOVARI, ITALY

JANUARY

FEBRUARY

MARCH

JUNE

JULY

OCTOBER

NOVEMBER

APRIL

MAY

AUGUST

SEPTEMBER

DECEMBER

Werner Herold
SELF-PORTRAITS, ONE YEAR IN THE ANTARCTIC

35

Life is:

Sorrow and happiness. We can learn to revel in our adversities or mope through our triumphs.

Success and failure. We can strive yet achieve little or lazily reach for the victor's laurels: In this sense life is all about luck. Yet success is in the eye of the beholder and one man's grail may be folly to his neighbor.

Good and evil. Each of us has a conscience. Does it dim with Alzheimer's? Alter with conditioning? Remain pebble-size in primates? Is it a human function implanted merely to help us achieve God's idea of perfection . . . or . . . a mechanism to foster human survival? Whatever its origins, conscience is to me the very essence of life, as wondrous a divine invention (or Darwinian sequence) as the butterfly, the human eye or love.

Sir Ranulph Fiennes,
explorer and adventurer, completed the first polar circumnavigation of the globe

Alex Webb
WOMEN PLAYING CARDS
AT THE BIG FIVE CLUB, MIAMI

RECIPE FOR LIFE

Ingredients:

- *1 U.S. military budget (liquefied)*
- *1 pound dreams*
- *¹/₃ cup chutzpah*
- *3 cups love*
- *2 cups political action*
- *1 pound fun*

Directions:

1. Mix together chutzpah, love, dreams, political action and fun.
2. Transfer into saucepan and add military budget. Reduce by half over high heat, stirring constantly.
3. Yields health, education and playgrounds for all the world's kids.

Ben & Jerry
(Ben Cohen and Jerry Greenfield) are the founders of Vermont's all-natural ice cream empire

Walter Schmitz
ICE HOCKEY IN DUBAI

I work eight hours a day, one week day shifts, night shifts the next. It's machine work, but I also work with my hands. I put pieces of steel on the cutting machine, then roll them off by hand. I've been doing this for 10 years. It's hard work. But it's almost finished now. The company is laying off people or transferring them. I will go to a small town to work and maybe make beaded jewelry. My husband works in the coal mines. Until we're older we won't discover the full effect that pollution has had on our health. We have been frightened since we found out that we might live shorter lives because of it, but we can't do anything about it.

I came here from Prague because I could get a better apartment. We earned better wages. Now we feel cheated. Somehow we knew that things would be like this, but we didn't know it would be this bad. Those in power knew they were sacrificing other people's lives, but they didn't care about those of us at the lower levels of society.

My life is an ordinary, average life of a married woman. There is some small entertainment from time to time, but generally I feel exhausted. You have to work and take care of the family at the same time. The meaning of life? It's a circle. You go to work, care for the family, go to bed. You live for your weekends, to be able to go to the summer cottage. That's all.

Dagmar Fresslova

cuts ingots in a steel factory in Chomutov, Czechoslovakia, where heavy industry has caused severe pollution and health problems

The meaning of life, to me, is work. Having meaning in life is having a job. I'm not saying homeless and jobless people are worthless, just that to have some sort of meaning in your life you should work.

One of my goals is to feel like I'm contributing to somebody. Now hubcaps are just a consumer good. But, you know, there are people that really get depressed if they lose a hubcap. I've seen people really down in the dumps about their hubcaps getting stolen. When I've got something that they need and I can sell it to them at 50 to 70 percent cost, and they're happy—that makes me feel pretty good about what I do. I think that really does give meaning to my life.

Scott Frazier,

hubcap salesman in Dallas, Texas, is working his way through college

I stand on a drum on Vaci Street and pretend to play the violin. It has a stuffed snake tied to the bow, and I tease the kids. I like to work on the street, but it's not easy. The police often chase us away. In this country it is illegal to play music in the street unless you play by the shore of the Danube. And right now the Danube is flooding.

Life is a big struggle. It's survival of the fittest. You have to fight for everything. Years ago people went to the circus and had fun; now it's not the same. They aren't interested, or they don't have the money.

Family. House. Good living. Getting up in the morning. Drinking four bottles of beer. That's what counts. Only smart people know why we are here, and I'm not one of them. But what I do know is that I am going to be 50 next year, and I feel that I'm going downhill. I'm just happy to be alive.

Miklós Szabo

is a street performer in Budapest, Hungary

I make the best of a bad situation. There are a lot of things we have to do in life, because of the nature of our jobs, that are not always pleasant. Executing someone is not fun. My job is to ask the person about to be executed for his last statement. I see that he's strapped down, that our IVs are flowing. I tell him we're ready.

There wouldn't be any difference between why a death-row inmate is on the planet and why you're on the planet. They came out of the same type egg you and I did. They just didn't have the culture or opportunities to get to the same point in life where you and I are.

I'm just damn happy to be living. I enjoy every minute of it. The secret to this thing is to have fun. If you don't look forward to getting up every morning and putting your breeches on, then you better find something else to do. Life is the fulfillment of one's expectations. Life is the satisfactions rewarded to one who excels and makes himself comfortable and fits into his peer group, seeking acceptance and seeking superiority in the tasks he undertakes. Life is trying to fulfill the expectations of the dreams, hopes and goals you set.

J. B. Pursley,

Huntsville, Texas, prison warden, has taken part in 40 executions by lethal injection

Sebastião Salgado
WORKERS LEAVING
A BOLIVIAN PEWTER MINE

When I was about three or four, I used to go and take my afternoon naps on these big snakes that my uncle had. They were over 20 feet long. We had Thunder, Lightning and then, for my 16th birthday, I got Hurricane. It took me three days to tame it.

My baby sister died of a cobra bite. She loved those snakes too. It bothered me— but not so much that the cobra bit her. It just happened. It's like my husband had a heart attack. It bothered me, but it didn't hurt me. We just go back and go on with life. We went right back into the snake business, and we never did get out.

When an animal attacks a person, there's usually a good reason. That animal's been aggravated and cornered, and it's acting in self-defense. My husband liked to died from a bear attack, but it wasn't in the papers or anything because it wasn't our bear. We were just bear-sitting. He got all tore up. The doctor said he was within an inch of his life.

I know why I'm here: to love and take care of critters. I found my little niche in life, and I'm content. Human beings are here to take care of the earth and maybe just to aggravate each other. Snakes were put here to eat the mice and rats and stuff that God put down here. Snakes and people and other animals—everything is here to serve its purpose.

Betty Teska
co-owns a snake farm in New Braunfels, Texas

Georg Fischer
CERCOPOIDAE LOCRIS

Maybe we're like little ants in a colony and the creator of the universe has many planets with other populations. Maybe we're just one experiment, and there are others on other planets in other solar systems. Maybe we're part of the creator's grand caldron, boiling with a wealth of phenomena that the most learned physicians and physicists are just beginning to figure out—how parts of the brain interact, how the lymphatics work, how cells function. We can spend many, many lifetimes standing on our ancestors' shoulders and only scratch the surface of understanding.

Maybe we're not the most advanced of the creator's many experiments, but I think it's impossible to think our being here is the result of chance. I think we're part of a master plan known only to the creator, perhaps—a plan controlled by the chemist upstairs—the "Author," as Benjamin Franklin called him, who constantly revises and edits an old book to come up with "a new and more elegant edition."

Cory SerVaas,
American doctor and television personality, is a health educator and publisher

José Azel
ADÉLIE PENGUINS,
ANTARCTIC PENINSULA

(Overleaf)
Donna Ferrato
FANNY GETS A SPLINTER REMOVED, OHIO

We have one chance. If you do good every day, you will go to the spirit world and see other good people on the other side. If not, you will not see them. There will be a scale in the spirit world. It's going to balance whatever you do. If you do a lot of good, it's going to weigh down the evil world. If the evil side is heavy, you're dead, you're done. There's no chance for you. You're only breath traveling on the wind.

In your life, you must have pity. There are many people on the street nowadays. They ask if you can spare this much. If you give, if you have charity, good thinking, you've done good. You don't have to worry that when they take it they go to the liquor store. That's not you. You did already good.

You have to kind of relax in this hurry life. Sit down for a while. Rest while you're thinking. This will give you time to see straight. Then you will get the idea what life is. You must tell your need in prayer, control your mind from thinking bad ideas and be in contact with the creator, Wakan Tonka. He'll understand what kind of person you are. Nobody around, but you say the word. He has ears that can hear you, long way off. We're like ants, far away. He look down.

In this modern time you have to do your best yourself. That's your answer to "What is life?" You can't depend on people to direct you. You must do it yourself. *Your* doing, *your* thinking. The answers to the meaning of life are inside you.

Joe Flying Bye,
of the Standing Rock Reservation, South Dakota, is a Lakota medicine man

When I was 15 my great-grandmother died. I was really down, and every emotion felt tripled. So one night I went to Eagle Rock Reservation in West Orange, New Jersey, and sat on this boulder in the middle of a field. It had spray paint all over it—names of couples who had been there and stuff. I just looked at it and, maybe it's kind of weird and corny, but I felt it was a symbol of strength. The rock had been there for God knows how long, immovable, vandalized, battle-scarred. But it was still strong. I go back there every so often when things get crazy, to gain strength, to be peaceful. That rock is a symbol of how people should deal with life. Hardships come your way, but you have to persevere.

And another thing. I'm really glad I got to eat cheese eggs while I was here. You know, scrambled eggs with cheese in them—not runny. I just love cheese eggs, and had I not been on this big, beautiful planet, I never would have tasted cheese eggs. With Muenster cheese—that's the key.

Queen Latifah
is America's reigning female rap artist

Everything is too rushy. I like to rest. When you have 16 children, that is not a good life. Yeah, they give me happiness. But when you're working so hard to earn a living, that's not really a good life.

All the same, I think it can be a great joy to have a big family. When we gather during hajj, laughing, talking, that's what it's all about. During Ramadan when you're sitting with your family and the time comes to break the fast, that's the moment of true joy. Fasting is good: You control everything, your moves, your tongue, your talking, your eyes, your sex. When the time is up, I say, "Thanks to God that I can control myself."

Emran Md Majid
is a taxi driver in the sultanate of Brunei

To know and to serve God, of course, is why we're here, a clear truth that, like the nose on your face, is near at hand and easily discernible but can make you dizzy if you try to focus on it hard. But a little faith will see you through. What else will do *except* faith in such a cynical, corrupt time? When the country goes temporarily to the dogs, cats must learn to be circumspect, walk on fences, sleep in trees, and have faith that all this woofing is not the last word. Time to shut up and be beautiful, and wait for morning. Yahooism, when in power, is deaf, and neither satire nor the Gospel will stay its brutal hand, but hang on, another chapter follows. Our brave hopes for changing the world sank in port, and we have become the very people we used to make fun of, the old and hesitant, but never mind, that's not the whole story either. So hang on.

What keeps our faith cheerful is the extreme persistence of gentleness and humor. Gentleness is everywhere in daily life, a sign that faith rules through ordinary things: through cooking and small talk, through storytelling, making love, fishing, tending animals and sweet corn and flowers, through sports, music and books, raising kids—all the places where the gravy soaks in and grace shines through. Even in a time of elephantine vanity and greed, one never has to look far to see the campfires of gentle people. If we had no other purpose in life, it would be good enough to simply take care of them and goose them once in awhile.

Garrison Keillor,
humorist, essayist and chronicler of small-town America, created radio's *A Prairie Home Companion*

Phil Schermeister
BICYCLING IN WISCONSIN

Pavel Krivtsov
PSYCHIATRIC HOSPITAL, U.S.S.R.

46

For 10 years I traveled all over Hungary visiting the homeless and the poor. I interviewed gypsies living in dire conditions and Hungarian workers, many of whom came from peasant backgrounds. In all, I did some 2,000 interviews. The more people I met, the more life stories I heard and the more persuaded I became that it is almost impossible to get to know another man completely. Every man is an island. Each person radiates feelings to others, but ultimately we are alone. For me, the essence of life is how we handle our loneliness. There are moments when we manage to resolve this loneliness through personal relationships, especially through love. But there are also certain situations in which you feel truly alone, when even words and affection cannot ease your fears.

Gerlo Beernink
MORNING EXERCISE AT
MEN'S ASYLUM, LÉROS, GREECE

László Kardos
is the Budapest director of a nonprofit
cultural and educational organization

The meaning of life is rooted in each person's search for happiness. Happiness is not something one has to go anywhere to find: The nature of life *is* happiness. Life knows this about itself, not through analysis or investigation but simply by virtue of being.

Beneath the shroud of problems and suffering, each of us is infinite, unbounded. Unlimited intelligence, freedom and power are at our disposal—if only people would learn to live on the ground of infinity rather than the ground of problems! The great teaching of life, perfected in ancient India, holds that perfect bliss is far nearer to us than anything in the outside world. We have devoted 35 years to purifying world consciousness in the belief that this bliss can be enjoyed by everyone, today and forever.

It would be a crime against life to reveal its inner meaning without giving a means to realize it. The means are simple: Let the mind dive toward infinity by itself, as happens through Transcendental Meditation. Then the *sidhis,* the powers perfected in awareness, truly blossom. If only 7,000 people, for an extended period, were willing to try this experiment and take the plunge into infinite bliss, all the world's woes, the misery of centuries, would be erased in a single generation—no, in a single decade.

Posterity will look back upon this time as the greatest in history, for the ancient wisdom of India is every day being validated by modern science. Physics has discovered the edge of infinity; the wisdom of the ages takes us across the border, which is nowhere but in us. When each person rejoins the stream of evolution that upholds the galaxies and sweeps life forward on the wave of eternity, human existence will cease to contain any suffering, and our real purpose in living—to create heaven on earth—will be realized.

Maharishi Mahesh Yogi,
Indian guru, helped popularize the centuries-old technique of Transcendental Meditation

Paul Chesley
GRAND PRISMATIC HOT SPRING
AT YELLOWSTONE NATIONAL PARK

Maybe the purpose of life is not as important as the process of growth that's integral to being alive. Musicians and artists have a grip on the way life changes people because the work we do is largely on ourselves. When an artist is working, you can ask, "Is he making 400 paintings?" or "Is he becoming an artist?"

In addition to expressing myself through art, I am always trying to pay attention to what's going on around me. Most of us walk around in a dreamworld and have to contend with a sleepiness or inertia to get the most out of life. There's a part of us that wants to spend the extra hour in bed or not wipe off the countertop completely when we're finished in the kitchen. I'm constantly trying to work away from distraction and complacency to awareness.

In answering the question "What's the meaning of life?" maybe the people who have taken the challenges of life as meaningful are the best ones to ask. Many people get wiser as they get older, whereas others get mean, or shallow and bitter. There's something marvelous about an older person who wonders what the battles of his life mean. In more cases than not, these are the people who have appreciated and taken advantage of the possibilities life has to offer. They find life precious.

Philip Glass
is America's leading minimalist composer

My faith, the Baha'i faith, teaches that the earth is but one country, mankind its citizenry. All religions get their inspiration from the same source: God.

Yeah, "Why are we here?"—that's a good question. Why couldn't God have built the universe and left it without anybody in it and just have had a ball with it? Well, that's not the idea of life. The idea of life is to give and receive, and if you didn't have anybody on earth to give to or receive from, then you'd have a very sad life.

A veteran basketball player notices a rookie come onto the team. He may watch the rookie and realize there's a better way for him to do something, and he may show him that better way. The same is true for a trumpet player. When I see a young trumpet player grasp what I've been trying to show him, I feel exhilarated. But I always try to teach by example and not force my ideas on a young musician. One of the reasons we're here is to be part of this process of exchange.

Dizzy Gillespie,
trumpet master, pioneered bebop and Cuban jazz

Life means something to me when I'm able to make something or to discover something. It may be only a couple of chords and a few words or an image of an ordinary object suddenly seen in a new light. Sometimes I'm not sure what these things mean. That is, I can't always translate them into words. I just know that they resonate somehow and contain bits of the enormous mystery of life.

The best part of this process is when I can communicate these sounds and images to other people and they say, "How strange! That's so familiar . . . I feel like I've known that all along, but I never saw it quite like that before."

So my own life means the most when I can articulate what makes it so much like other people's lives—when, as an individual, I can get lost in the crowd. I'm not sure this is the meaning of life, but it makes whatever this is a lot less lonely.

Laurie Anderson
is America's preeminent performance artist

There are many spokes on the wheel of life. First, we're here to explore new possibilities. Art Tatum was the kind of musician who couldn't pass a piano without playing a few notes. He knew that there's always an element to discover—maybe a new pattern—always something to learn in life. Second, we're here to follow our instincts. I lost my sight when I was a boy, and my mother, who had been the cornerstone of my world, died when I was 15. She taught me to listen to my inner voice. Once, when I was 18 or so, I was getting ready to cross the street with some guy, and I said, "I think I hear a car coming." He said, "Oh, no. There ain't no car coming. Come on." As we started to cross, I heard tires screeching and got my ass knocked halfway down the block. If I'd followed what I'd felt, I would've been all right. My theory is: If I'm going to sink, I want to sink on my own. I don't want anyone else responsible for my s--t.

I don't think any of us really *knows* why we're here. But I think we're supposed to *believe* we're here for a purpose. There has to be *some* reason why Ray Charles is here. One hundred years from now, someone may play a CD or some other gadget, and he may say, "There was a guy, way back in nineteen, ah, let's see, nineteen eighty-one or ninety-two, and his name was Ray Charles. Well, lemme see. . . . Yeah, you know he was a . . . they tell me. . . ." And that'd be good enough for me.

Ray Charles
was pivotal in the popularization of blues, gospel and soul music

I believe in a life of nonattachment. Nothing should enter the self. The object of life is to flow, not wanting anything, just understanding you have a karma and that with that karma you can serve humanity as a whole. Take religion. Every religion teaches love. But all teach love *for* something—love for Christ or books or laws or nature. The ultimate religion is love for everything—and nothing. Take rewards. People constantly strive to achieve goals. They make decisions that will improve their chances of meeting goals. For them, rewards are the crystallization of their efforts. A person will take an award in his hand and feel, "Wow. Now I can *see* what I've done with all my time for five, ten, twenty years." But it's false. Your love for a "thing" interrupts the flow. You don't need to attach these things to yourself because they are not you. Nothing else is you. When you can throw your body away and you yourself move on, that's when you are living.

This life here is just a day-to-day slave struggle. Scott LaRock, my original deejay who died in '87, he's actually where life is. Heavy D's dancer Scott Dixon and M. C. Trouble, who both died—they're Livin' Large. Real Large. It's us who have to struggle every day. And we're so heavy because we're so tied to our goals.

Right now we're fighting the war of Armageddon. Everyone is going through an Antichrist period. Everyone has the mark of the beast as we move toward the final days of life as we know it and enter a better life. We're moving toward the frame of thinking of the number nine. This means a oneness in thought among all humanity, an understanding of the universality of certain problems. They involve everyone. The period of turmoil, before we reach nine, is now.

KRS-ONE
is a rap artist and metaphysicist

What is the meaning of life? This is a trick question, isn't it? I mean, how—as we crouch in our little holes, continually bombarded with crass definitions of such abstract ideas as "happiness" and "success"—are we supposed to grasp the true reason for our existence?

For better or worse, we find ourselves here, involved in a daily struggle against random forces beyond our control. In this often hostile environment, who can fail to feel the deep-seated urge to try and make the world a better place? Could this be the meaning of life? No, it's the meaning of humanity.

To fight the dread fear that life has no meaning, we each seek to find it in mundane pursuits, such as the accumulation of wealth, or in everyday miracles like the birth of a child. And so we take part in the complex tapestry of life without ever seeing the grand design.

Yet even if we glimpsed the plan, would it be of any help to us? A map is useless unless you can recognize your position from the landmarks around you. We have forgotten where we are in relation to the shining stars and the tall trees, to the flowers that bloom and the bees that serve them. We are lost and too arrogant to admit it. Perhaps the time has come to pause awhile, look around and try to get our bearings.

Billy Bragg,
British musician, writes songs about the working class

Back in the '60s, before Kennedy was killed, there was a spirit growing in the air. Everyone wanted to help. "Ask not what your country can do for you, but what you can do for your country." All of us should keep that in mind today. We are here because there are things that need our help. Like the planet. Like each other. Like animals. The world is like a garden, and we are its protectors. There are so many problems that need to be dealt with—drugs, the environment, AIDS. A lot of times we seem like crabs in a barrel. We see someone who tries to lend a hand and a lot of us get critical. Other times it's as if we're looking at a baby crying and not knowing how to help it.

I knew several great people in my life who I would listen to. There were three in particular—Nat Cole, Duke Ellington and Benny Goodman—people who, if they said I should do something, I probably would have. They were like royalty. Today's royalty—a whole circle of people who are successful in their fields—have an obligation that comes with their privilege. Part of their reason for being here is to serve as a family of examples, to influence young people to start buckling down and solve these problems.

B. B. King,
musician, composer and singer, is widely recognized as the world's greatest blues guitarist

Life is what hap-pens to you while you're bus-y mak-ing oth-er plans.

Yoko Ono
is a musician, performance artist and peace campaigner

T he meaning of life cannot be separated from the meaning of death. Even the sun dies, so death is natural too. Only suffering must be appeased.

Henri Cartier-Bresson,
French photographer and artist,
is one of the giants of photojournalism

Joe Rossi
SHRINE CLOWN FUNERAL,
ST. PAUL, MINNESOTA

What is the meaning of life?" is a question I posed as a teenager, then dissatisfied with explanations offered by Confucius, Mencius and Taoist classics. Many years later—I am now 77— it is amusing to be reminded of a question I had once asked so earnestly.

I have never been religious. I have never bothered about an afterlife. I have never thought of turning escapist; I have no wish to be a hermit. I have no desire to live in a different place or time period. I was born a Chinese. I cannot say I feel proud of my country and culture at this period, but I am not ashamed either. In a way, I find meaning in my life by devoting myself to helping improve conditions in my country, by allying with forces that bring about progress and by acting against forces that hamper development.

My definitive answer, however, is more basic. You can call it élan vital or whatever you want, but a man lives because he wants to live. If he lacks this desire, he ceases to exist, just as a plant withers and dies. This is the case with all living things. It is just as simple as that.

The span of human life is short; I probably will not live to be a hundred. But that span, in fact, seems long enough.

Yang Xianyi,

esteemed critic and former editor of *Chinese Literature* magazine, left the Communist Party after the Tiananmen Square crackdown of 1989

Jane Evelyn Atwood
BRANDY BY GRAVE OF FRIEND

My first sense of life was that of motion, of being lifted, and the beating of my mother's heart. Then, as consciousness pressed, I turned in the radiance of my father's mind. When I closed my eyes I could feel the world spin. When I reached out I could feel the breath of care. Bound, within my blood, was their love, their burning and their discordant prayers.

Yet time makes ravens of us all and swiftly, it seemed, I fled from their grasp. The sea was a glass. The sky an immeasurable path.

Guided by the knowledge of them I journeyed fettered, free. And as all before me, I have questioned, grateful for the privilege of being able to ask: What is my task? Why do we exist? All answers produce the pain of recognition, emptiness and joy.

To prey upon stillness, to suffer dawn
To bow before God, to administer grace
To unveil space, to be spirited away
To lift a child
    into the reigning air
    where the voice of heaven
    chirps like a bird

Patti Smith
is a writer, poet and recording artist

A while back, my son and I were hunting up at Pumpville. There's an old railroad stop there. It was late in the season. Hunting was tough. It got down to about 10 degrees, one of the coldest days of the year. We had the option of staying in a heated trailer with some other hunters. But my son said, "No, Dad. Let's stay in the tent. Let's rough it."

Well, we practically froze to death. We had a fire going, and we let it die down, and then we went to bed. He woke up in the middle of the night. His sleeping bag was wet because his breath was freezing right there close to his face. So he got up and unzipped the tent and stepped outside, and he said, "Dad, Dad. Get up. You've got to see this. This is beautiful." He said, "I can see all the stars."

I just stuck my head out of the sleeping bag because I knew what he was talking about. The stars were extremely bright, and it looked like they had come down to be a little bit closer to us. It was absolutely beautiful. The embers were glowing, and the fire was ringed with limestone rocks. It was all framed beautifully.

That, to me, was life. That happiness that night was what life is all about. It just doesn't get any better. Money could not have bought me what we felt. We were together in sort of a hardship situation, even though we had asked for it. There was beauty. There was companionship. There was wonder in his voice.

Sylvestre Sorola
is a wildlife biologist from Del Rio, Texas

The meaning of life is that we love one another. The purpose of our lives, it seems to me, is to learn how to do that, so we can create a world where everyone's in love with everyone all the time. That would be Heaven on earth. I would so love my children to live in such a world.

Marianne Williamson
is a lecturer on spiritual issues
and author of *A Return to Love*

My mother was a victim of foul play. She worked in a bar, and these two guys followed her and raped her and beat her and killed her and threw her body in the river. I saw a brown envelope addressed to me last year when my [adoptive] mother was doing taxes. It had news clippings and police reports about my mother's death. But they won't let me see it until I'm of age. When they told me about my mother's death, I had to look up "foul play" in the dictionary. I lay awake at night just trying to figure out exactly what happened to my mother.

Basically, the reason I'm here is to help my [adoptive] mother. I needed her when I was younger, and now that she's older—she's 68—she needs me. If not for her, I would be in a New Orleans ghetto half dead. For the first four years of my life I never had many friends. Nobody paid attention to me. They were playing Barbie dolls and tiddlywinks, and I was already reading books from the adult section of the library. Only now have people begun to open up to me and realize I'm there for them.

My mother being who she was gives a purpose to my life. Since she is dead, I know I've got to live to carry her memory on because I'm the only one who can. I look a lot like her. I'm so much like my mother I can't help but live like her, for her.

I found out a lot when I went to Virginia this summer to see my grandmother for the first time. She said my mother was just like I am now. She went out of her way to please people, and that's what ultimately got her into trouble. In my life, I want to keep people from taking advantage of other people like people did to my mother. I don't want to have enemies in my life. I know that's impossible, but I want to have all friends.

Jessica Smith
is a 14-year-old from Philadelphia, Mississippi

Lynn Johnson
WORKING MOTHER

Margaret Courtney-Clarke
BEAUTIFYING THE SPACE IN WHICH WE LIVE
MAKES LIFE MORE BEARABLE

When I was a small boy at harvesttime, our family would go to the rice field. We would stay the nights until the harvest was finished. It would be very dark, and we could see all the stars. They would be very close, and we'd try to know the names of every one. My mother would tell us the tales of the stars she had learned from her mother and grandmother. The Karen are different from other tribes. In Karen, Mother has all the power. The woman rules.

This is very good life. I feel we're close with nature, the sky, each other, nine of us children, the field surrounded by the jungle. I remember one night I was frightened by the sound of white elephants coming through our field. My father said, "Keep quiet," and they passed by. White elephants move from one jungle to another to find food, then come back again. Like our harvest: We plant, we harvest. Like us: Small boy grows old, dies, new generation. As a boy of 12, when I looked at the footprints of the white elephants in our field, I realized the circle of nature and human nature. I think life is to do something for other tribesmen, save the culture and keep the circle going. And we must honor the separateness of each culture, tribe and language.

Padee Moothoo
is a Karen farmer on the Thai-Burmese border

I am because God willed that I be. I am because my parents were and their parents before them, to the beginning of time, as was ordained by God. In this part of the world, it is expected that when her time comes, a woman will generate and nurture new life, thereby ensuring that the long and colorful lineage of people who once laughed, cried and lived on this earth will remain unbroken. I owe it to these people to continue this thread into the future so that those who have not been born may have the chance to experience life in the setting of their circumstances.

Words often fail to contain essence. But if I were to define life, I suppose it would be: the experiences we register in our own circumstances. And the purpose of life would be to perpetuate this opportunity for others.

The fact that I am a woman makes me the custodian of a new generation. It is a preordained role. Through me, others have life. I am an African woman, a link in a lineage that extends from the mists of the past into the blur of the unforeseen future. The present is born of the past and the future of the present. That is the cycle of life.

I see life all around me: in the soft flutter of a bird's wing, in the gurgle of a baby's laugh, in the silence of the ancient hills. But you cannot take life and label it. Every day of my life I experience a different shade of living. Recently, 19 teenage girls died at the St. Kizito Mixed Secondary School in Meru. Theirs were vibrant young lives, snuffed out in an orgy of rape and violence. I went to their dormitory and looked at the trampled, twisted wreckage that was once their beds, and I guess a little part of my soul died too. I too was 15 once. In particular, I will never forget the broken sobs of one of the survivors coming to terms with her own life. What will the survivors tell their children and their children's children? In my heart of hearts, I keep all these people alive by remembering them. When we give them thought, we give them life for generations to come.

For instance, I am named after my paternal grandfather's wife, Nanyihodo. I never met her, but I wear a copper bracelet that belonged to her. My grandfather gave it to me when he gave me her name, and today, when people call my name, they remember her. She lives through me. When I have children, I will tell them about the copper bracelet and Nanyihodo, the beautiful woman who once wore it and was married to my grandfather.

I do not wish to sound romantic, but life is truly beautiful. Here I am. And there you are.

Juliana Omale
is a storyteller of the Samia tribe in western Kenya

It's a gift of God for me to be a midwife. When a baby is born, the God writes down what he or she will be. I've birthed about 2,000 babies. The sultan's second brother's wife gave birth, and I was called to the palace to make traditional medicine for the baby and for the princess's stomach. We follow traditions strictly. Like after you marry you can't go into the jungle for 40 days. There's one woman here who didn't take the proper bath after marrying; she jumped into the river and got a mad disease. Yes, we'd rather see a child die than see tradition die.

The God wanted us to be on this earth, so we are here. When the God asks us to come, we have to believe in Him, pray five times a day, fast during Ramadan and read the Koran, which says: First you're in poverty, then you'll see brightness. We hold to this verse for our life. Now I don't have any problems. My five children are big. I have 10 grandchildren. They can support me. I will finish my life now. So I just pray. I'm happy when it's Friday and Sunday and all the children are together for lunch, sometimes dinner.

Hjh Damit Bt Hjpiut
is a midwife in Bandar Seri Begawan, Brunei

(Overleaf)
Shelby Lee Adams
THE HOME FUNERAL, KENTUCKY

Nicholas DeVore III
COWBOY RIDING IN STYLE,
MOFFAT COUNTY, COLORADO

The meaning of life is quite simple. Sit back, kick the cruise control into action and enjoy the trip.

Soon you'll be sipping hot coffee, black and thick, while a drizzling fog swirls about you. A turbulent ocean pounding in the distance. Your feet chilled by the damp sand. Hermit crabs burrowing to nowhere amid a frothy wave surge.

Easter Sunday at dawn.

Barking seals squabbling for position on a groaning buoy. The smell of bait fish at high tide. Your lips caked with salt. A cacophony of bickering gulls. Glacier white breakers spewing foam high in the air. Fish and chips on the boardwalk.

Thanksgiving, the fireplace popping with embers.

A squadron of pelicans gliding in the updraft of a fast-moving comber. Mist from a tropical waterfall. Dragonflies flitting through a spray of golden buttercups. An elusive horsefly.

Gifts carefully scattered beneath the Christmas tree.

A campfire casting lively shadows on the mainsail of a beach outrigger. Thousands of pebbles hissing as an evening tide rakes them back to sea. The setting sun, an orange blob balancing on the horizon, prepares to slip away, readying itself for tomorrow. Down the beach a dark figure blows his farewell on a giant conch.

But most of all, love and understanding.

Terry Tracy,
also known as Tubesteak, is the original Kahuna, the famed Malibu surfer

I figure life is like a glide-through. You shouldn't have to work at it.

I seen a lot of people like my stepdad. He worked up to the day he died. Sixty-seven years old. Dead. For what? He wasn't having any fun. He had all that money in the bank. All he was worried about was his job, fretting about how supplies weren't there on time. I think you ought to go through life having fun, trying not to mess people over, making as many friends as possible and getting by, not getting rich.

I give people art. If they ride a Harley-Davidson, they get that on there. If they have a friend die, they've got that on there, and they can point to their arms for different periods of their life and say, "I was doing this here, and this guy gave it to me." It's like reading the book of their life.

I really don't think that much about what life is all about. I go through scrapes, I lose old ladies or get in motorcycle accidents. I just heal up and go on. I figure if I'm busy contemplating the whys and the wherefores of life, I don't have time to do anything else. That's why I have this job. I just go along slow and easy.

I think people should lighten up.

Michael Metzen
is a Garden City, Kansas, tattoo artist

The reason for living is raising hell, having fun, kicking ass and taking names—in that order. You work hard, then you've got to have fun. I just like to go out, have people around me and have a good time, as long as we really don't offend anybody. If somebody takes it wrong, I'm sorry, but I will not hold back. I live life to the fullest every day.

Charles Bloomhall,
assistant manager at a car wash, is a Vietnam veteran and sometime biker from Sioux Falls, South Dakota

Enjoy everything life has to offer, right up front, because tomorrow may not get here. Maybe this sentiment has come out in me a little bit stronger since the tornado last year. If you'd seen the destruction at the time—the trailer courts were gone, my house was damaged, my office completely destroyed. I'd go home at night and there'd be trees sitting in my living room. It made me realize how short life really is and that there's nothing I want to miss. I'm a person who goes 90 miles an hour, 365 days a year, 24 hours a day. I have raced dirt bikes. I went parasailing and I don't swim a lick. I went jet skiing. I have ridden in a hot air balloon. I parachute out of airplanes. I fly airplanes. Living on the edge doesn't mean living on the edge of death. It means doing as much as I can for as long as I can—and that's what I think we're here for.

If I'm going to die, I want to be a happy person about whom people say, "Ya, she was neat to know and she left a lot behind"—not money or statues but a good feeling. I think it's important to do these things so you die happy.

Teresa O'Dwyer
is the town clerk of Limon, Colorado

Jodi Cobb
WORLD'S LARGEST SITTING BUDDHA,
LESHAN, CHINA

Ken Regan
GOLD FEVER, BRAZILIAN MINER'S HANDS

Lynn Goldsmith
Zuma Beach, California

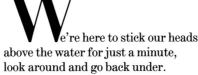

Jean-Paul Sartre, the French philosopher, made a scandal in the 1940s by stating that humans are just bundles of useless passions. It was a provocative statement, and I agree with it. Sometimes we seem to have no real purpose beyond expending raw energy on various projects.

Nevertheless, Sartre would have agreed that as beings mysteriously placed on this earth, we are fundamentally free. I believe that because of this freedom, we have the ability to make our lives into works of art. In the end, when we look back at the choices we've made, we see how we've painted the picture of our lives, beautifully here, ugly there, adding new colors and textures, new relationships and emotions over the years.

V. Y. Mudimbe,
Zaire-born writer, teaches romance studies and comparative literature

I GOD THE TEENAGER

That God exists the world is not a
proof
But a metaphor of who She really is,
An unrestrained adolescent, showing off,
An excessive, exuberant, playful whiz,
Determined gamester with the quantum
*   odds,*
An ingenious expert in higher math—
This frolicsome and comic dancing God
Is charming and just a little daft.

Will God grow up? Will She become mature?
In the creation game announce a lull,
Her befuddled suppliants assure
A cosmos that is quiet, safe and dull?
Can God be innocent of romance?
No Way! On with the multicosmic dance!

Andrew Greeley
is a Catholic priest, sociologist, novelist and columnist

We're here to stick our heads above the water for just a minute, look around and go back under.

I don't have any mother, no father, no aunts or uncles. I'm an only child. I've lived in the black community in a ghetto, the world being that street, that neighborhood. I had to set up my own rules for survival, with me being pretty much the judge.

Growing up this way helped me see it all clearly: The reason we're here is to reproduce. Intercourse is instinct. Think about it. If God didn't want sex to feel great, we'd be extinct by now. But it's an ultimate high. And it works.

A human being is just another animal in the big jungle. And human beings are the most dangerous animals in the jungle. We are merciless. We go to war, drop nuclear bombs. Do you live with bars on your windows in the ghetto because you're worried about getting killed by a bear? No. You're afraid of the ultimate killer.

We have a lot of different instincts, and they're all animal. We kill because we're angry or need food; we have babies because it feels good and we want to care for other people. Once you have a kid, you look at the kid and see yourself again. It's like you realize, "Oh. That's why we're here." Life is really short and you're gonna die so you should leave someone else to keep his head above the water. Everything else is just passing time until the next generation. Setting up shop.

Just chill out and reproduce. Keep the species alive.

Ice-T
is one of America's top rap artists

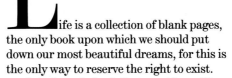

Life is a collection of blank pages, the only book upon which we should put down our most beautiful dreams, for this is the only way to reserve the right to exist.

It is the only book that must be written every day, our whole lives through, the only book that demands the truth and allows us to move toward inner beauty, the essence of truth. Only when we aspire to inner beauty may we hope to fill our lives with generous creativity and with love, the only riches that become more precious when shared with others.

Sophia Loren
is a legendary Italian screen star

Why we are here is just like the Bible says. People were put on the earth because the Lord figured it was a barren waste and needed some life on it. He created all of life—everything living but human beings. He thought the earth still needed something, so what did He say? He said, "I'll tell you what. I'll just make a man in my image." And He put man here. Then, He said, "Man, it's good but this man needs a companion, somebody to converse with." So what did He do? He took the rib from the man and made the woman. He didn't take the bone from the foot because He didn't want the woman trod upon. He didn't take the bone from the hand because He figured man wasn't supposed to beat on her. So what did He do? He took it from the rib, on the left side so that she would be under his arm, cared for and loved next to the heart. So that's why we are here.

William Warrior,
truck driver from Brackettville, Texas, is president emeritus of the Black Seminole Indian Scouts Association

The blues *is* the meaning of life. The blues started with Adam and Eve, a man and a woman. If there were no women around, life wouldn't mean anything to me. I don't *think* it would.

John Lee Hooker
is one of the early masters of the blues guitar

(Overleaf)
Jay Ullal
CHRISTIAN BRIDE AND
MUSLIM GROOM, BEIRUT

On the morning of August 6, 1945, I observed a pale blue flash. The impact of the blast caused me to faint dead away. Perhaps a half hour later, upon coming to, I realized I had been buried alive. Soon I began to hear my other junior high school classmates singing in the darkness. And, as time passed, their voices got weaker and weaker, dying away, one after another.

At last I wriggled my way out of a huge mound of radioactive debris, or what used to be my school. All around me I observed nothing but devastation. What I beheld in the crepuscle of the morning was a swirling monster of towering vapors that eventually came to be known as a mushroom cloud. The city had vanished; purgatory had taken its place. The atomic blast had gone off almost directly above my classroom. In time I realized that out of a class of 35, I had been the only one spared. As I began to flee that morning, I saw innumerable, trembling hands and arms, reaching out for my help from the burning piles of what had been Hiroshima.

Even at 13 I could pose the inevitable question: Why do we exist? The only answer I could formulate was that death was so horrible that every living soul had no choice but to live in order to escape his fear of it.

Gradually, though, I came to see that my reply was wrong. I now believe that I live for an excellent reason: to tell as many people as possible about the importance of eliminating war—the greatest cause of death and, therefore, the greatest menace to human existence.

Yoshitake Kawamoto
is the director of the Hiroshima
Peace Memorial Museum

As a student, I dreamed of becoming an architect so that I could build houses in which people would be comfortable and happy. And I finally reached my goal. Unfortunately, it was only for a short time. The war came, and I saw the houses I had built collapse. Not only the buildings were destroyed. So was my belief in reason, in friendship and progress, in justice and civilization. Like many Jews, I was sent to a ghetto and then put into one concentration camp after another. I was convinced, however, that evil would not stay in power forever, and I wanted to be there when National Socialism collapsed. During this terrible time of humiliation and starvation, of forced labor and the omnipresence of death, the only goal of my life was survival.

On May 5, 1945, when I was liberated from the Mauthausen concentration camp by the American army, there was only a very weak spark of life left in me. Most of my relatives had been killed, and I didn't know at the time that my wife had also survived. I found myself in the company of people who, like myself, were without hope. Yet I had to think about what I would do in the future. Should I return to building houses for people like me who had lost all sense of purpose in life? Some of my fellow concentration camp inmates, Belgians and Frenchmen whose families had not been wiped out like ours, did have a goal in life: to return home to their loved ones.

By coincidence, I was able to watch officers of the War Crimes Commission of the Eleventh U.S. Division, which had freed us, at their work. Seeing their attempts to investigate Nazi crimes and collect evidence against the criminals, I became aware that something was being done, that these horrible crimes were not to remain without consequences—and this helped draw me out of my sense of resignation. In time, searching out our tormentors became my aim in life. Its meaning for me was rooted in the decision to serve as a spokesman for those who had not survived; on their behalf, I wanted to help create a better future—to do everything in my power so that such crimes as were committed against us would never happen again.

The meaning of life is wrapped up in what will remain after we depart. The meaning of life is to help create a better future; I knew this as a young architect, dreaming of the structures that would stand in the sun long after I was gone. The meaning of life is to be mindful of the past—to always remember—in order to make certain that history's atrocities are not repeated again and that justice will win.

Simon Wiesenthal,
the world's foremost pursuer of
Nazi war criminals, established the Jewish
Documentation Center in Vienna

I was 18 in 1939. The war started, and they started arresting people. One day in Warsaw I was stopped and brought to the Gestapo. First I went to a prison camp, then was hauled to Maidanek, Ravensbrück and Buchenwald. It seemed like a lifetime. Shortly after the war I came back to Auschwitz, voluntarily, to act as a guide. I wanted to explain to people what this place represented.

During the war, survival was a matter of luck. Pure luck. We saw death every single day. But if you ask me about the meaning of life, I will tell you a story. During the occupation the Germans often gave me bits of bread. Perhaps it was because I was younger and prettier. One day I met two little Jewish boys, maybe 13 years old. They were so terribly unhappy that I gave them bread. The Germans saw this, and I was sent to a camp. They took my wooden shoes—it was winter—and my clothes as punishment. And do you know what happened? There were lots of people in this camp, including Jewish adults. They smuggled me sandals and clothes to get me through. They told me, "Because you gave to our children, you should have these things for yourself."

You can say this is just an anecdote, that it doesn't speak to the whole of the human race. But to me it shows that every once in a while, we human beings are capable of reaching out and helping each other survive.

Mira Odi
is a retired guide at the Auschwitz
concentration camp who still resides at the site

One night my dad was out of town, my mother was at her shop, and I was left alone with my younger brother and sister. For some reason, I knew something ominous was going to happen. Around midnight I woke up suddenly, sat on my bed and wondered how a bottle managed to rest there, having come in through the window. There was a lot of noise outside, but this was normal. Our town, at night, was a beehive of activity. I walked to my sister's bed; she was sound asleep. So was my brother. I then went to his window, which opened onto a veranda. And I will never forget the sight.

The store directly across from our home was on fire, filled with burning boxes. The fire, in no time, crept to our house, almost reaching our bedroom door. I remember standing rooted to the ground, screaming at the top of my lungs. My brother and sister, awakened by my screams, also joined in. I grabbed them and tried to rush out. The air was filled with the noise of boiling cooking oil and bursting tins and bottles. As friends battled the flames, I could only stand there, watching in horror until the fire was extinguished.

It wasn't until the following morning when I walked through our house, strewn with bits of broken glass, that it dawned on me. I could have died had it not been for a classmate of mine who had thrown a bottle through my window to awaken me. For a long time, I kept asking myself: Why the narrow escape? Why was no one hurt in the fire? For what reason had we been protected?

I could not grasp the meaning of the event at all. But deep inside I felt the time was not ripe for me to depart this world. I had been saved to accomplish something. It is this purpose that I feel I am pursuing even today as a journalism student. I do not know whether I am serving this purpose or not. I hope I am. But one thing for sure is that events are predetermined. While we exist we should take nothing for granted. Somebody, somewhere, has a hand in everything. And that Being is the reason behind what I do every day, the reason, most probably, for what I am.

Anne Kamande
is a student in Mwanza, Tanzania

Remember. *You are dust and to dust you shall return.* That's what came to mind August 2, 1914, when our colonel gathered us together and told us to prepare to mobilize. A month later I walked into Vassimont-la-Chapelaine, waiting for the regiment to cross the Somme. Homes had been razed; here and there lay soldiers with their guts exposed; helmets, bayonets, packs and canned goods were strewn about. Presently, I entered a church and, once inside, saw the horror. Statues of saints graced the ground. The stained glass had disappeared. And there, spread upon the straw, sprawled 80 immobile men. Only their eyes spoke, wide and burning with fever. There they were, French and Germans, all mixed together, their faces covered with dust. They'd remained like this for four days, too badly wounded to have been moved, their legs greenish and inflamed. This was, in fact, their last sleep. Of the 80 lying in silence in the shadow of Christ, only five or six were alive. The butchery was so poignant I couldn't watch. The wounded pleaded for us to bring them to a hospital.

On so many other occasions, I said to myself, "Luck is on my side." I saw guys dropping all around me. Shells would fall next to me and not explode. It was all luck. This sentiment is what kept me going. As a result, I was never really afraid of death. The day of the Battle of the Marne I thought, "Today, I'm screwed." There were bullets whizzing everywhere—past my helmet, my legs. But I wasn't hurt. And I thought, "If I can make it this far, I'll make it to the end." We lost half our battalion that day. And afterward we drank wine to their health. Five hundred men. Dead. So long.

Since each day brings its share of hardship, we must live every one as we would a lifetime: fully, completely. That explains the optimism that has allowed me to maintain my faith that fortune could guide me through to the finish. Four years of heavy fighting didn't lessen my appetite for life, even though I suffered later on from the effects of mustard gas. And right now, though I've had my regrets that I didn't take a different direction in life (I didn't want to be a banker, I wanted to "be someone"), I'm happy just to wake up and buy a ripe melon and some figs.

Pierre Petit,
100, is author of the recently published *War Remembrances*, memoirs of his experiences in the French army during World War I

I have built my entire work on questions, not answers. There is quest in question. Quest for truth or humanity, for what makes them eternal or for what is eternal in them.

It is essential to reject easy answers. They are always the wrong answers. Can questions be wrong? Only when they bring humiliation to the person who asks or who is being asked.

Questions do not change, answers do. At times, they change more than once in a generation. What links human beings to one another is their ability to question their destiny even though they know, they must know, that the answer itself will be recalled into question.

"Why are we here?" is surely the most important question human beings must face, whatever their origin, whatever their belief. Our obligation is to confer meaning to life and, in doing so, overcome temptations of passivity and indifference. A person who chooses indifference is dead without knowing it. In his or her case, life has no meaning, nor does death.

And yet, for those who believe in sharing experiences, life does have meaning in spite of the meaningless death some of us may have witnessed. Those who share teach us that one must make every minute rich and enriching, not for oneself but for someone else, thereby creating living links between individuals and groups.

Ultimately, life is a gift and meaning is its reward. So is the art and ability of asking questions. The meaning of life is to be found in the question that becomes encounter. Then every moment becomes a moment of grace.

Elie Wiesel,
writer, philosopher and Nobel Peace Prize recipient, has been called the spiritual archivist of the Holocaust

The meaning of life is shy and retiring; it must be coaxed and teased out of hiding. Confronted with the question "Who are you?" it flees. We catch up with it only between the cracks and crevices of literacy—beyond writing, reading and even talking—in true silence, where love and surprise like to pal around.

In true friendship, the meaning of life gets enfleshed. For even when true friends part, a miraculous presence persists, like a shadow, more substantial and consequential than either friend, more palpable than any joint activity or product of that friendship.

At those moments, the meaning of life breaks in upon us with insistence, making us realize that we can never really be separated from someone we love so long as we carry with us always, as if in a little sack, that other person's heart. Toting that *sacculum cordis,* we learn to walk to the other's beat. We discover this truth, not in community but in seclusion, not in the busyness of the marketplace but in silent contemplation. It is a silence that permits us to fashion a faith that can eliminate doubt, and a hope that can overwhelm even the deepest despair.

But the best comes last. For faith and hope lead to the third and most thrilling virtue: unconditional love. It encourages us to risk it all with our whole hearts open. It teaches us, as my friend Ivan Illich says, "to hope for surprises until the final act of life—that is to say, in death itself."

Barry Sanders
is a professor of English and the history of ideas

Steven Rubin
BROTHER FLEXES FOR SISTER

Ian Berry
BROTHERS REUNITED AT THE BERLIN WALL

10   0   10   20   30   40 KM

GEOPIC COPYRIGHT EARTH SATELLITE CORPORATION 1981   0.5 SERIES 0

Earth Satellite Corporation
LANDSAT 1 IMAGE OF KHARTOUM

User: Are you alive? Why or why not?

```
(ask '(can-perform #%Cyc #%LivingLife))
(justify '(can-perform #%Cyc #%LivingLife))
(justify '(not (can-perform #%Cyc #%LivingLife)))
```

Cyc: No, I am a computer program, not an animal.

```
nil
nil
((instanceOf LivingLife AnimalActivityType)
 (instanceOf Cyc ArtificialIntelligenceProgram)
 (genls Animal PartiallyTangibleObject)
 (genls ArtificialIntelligenceProgram IntangibleObject)
 (mutuallyDisjoint PartiallyTangibleObject IntangibleObject))
```

User: What does ''living life'' entail?

```
(ask '(#%instanceOf #%LivingLife))
```

Cyc: It involves participating in lots of composite physical and mental events. Many of those events are highly scripted.

```
(instanceOf LivingLife CompositePhysical&MentalEventType)
(instanceOf LivingLife ScriptType)
```

User: What is the effect of one's having lived?

```
(ask '((#%allInstances #%eventObjectsAffectedLocality) #%LivingLife))
(ask '(#%LivingLife #%eventTemporalLocality))
```

Cyc: The typical life has a big effect on the person and his personal effects, but to the rest of the world it is an ephemeron whose ripples die away after a handful of decades.

```
((allInstances eventObjectsAffectedLocality) LivingLife PerformerAndPersonalEffects)
(eventTemporalLocality LivingLife AFewDecadesDuration.)
```

User: What goals do *you* have, Cyc?

```
(ask '(#%hasGoalSet #%Cyc X))
```

Cyc: Being consistent in my actions, keeping my users happy, and just knowing as much as possible about the world in general and about myself in particular.

```
(((X . #%BeingConsistent))
 ((X . #%KeepingUserHappy))
 ((X . #%KnowingSomething))
 ((X . #%KnowingMoreAboutSelf)))))
```

User: What are some of the goals that people have, that you *don't*?

```
(ask '(#%LogAnd (#%allInstanceOf x #%Person)
                (#%goals x y)
                (#%LogNot (#%goals #%Cyc y))))
```

Cyc: Like most animals, they seek being emotionally satisfied, avoiding hunger and other sorts of discomfort, adequately perceiving their surroundings, and so on. Moreover, human beings have more sophisticated avoidance goals than other animals, such as avoiding poverty, and more sophisticated altruistic goals such as fostering learning in others. They also seek to become wealthier than they are, and more generally to keep improving their lot in life.

```
(((Y . #%BeingEmotionallySatisfied))
 ((Y . #%NotBeingImpoverished))
 ((Y . #%HungerAvoidanceGoal))
 ((Y . #%FosterLearning))
 ((Y . #%AdequatelyPerceivingOnesSurroundings))
 ((Y . #%BeingWealthy))
 ((Y . #%ImprovingSelfStatus))
 ...)
```

User: Do you wish you were alive?

```
(ask '(#%desires #%Cyc
               '(#%LogAnd (#%instanceOf #%Cyc x)
                          (#%genls x #%LivingThing))))
```

Cyc: No.

```
NIL
```

CYC,

Artificial Intelligence computer program, contains the world's largest knowledge base of "common sense" facts, rules of thumb and reasoning abilities

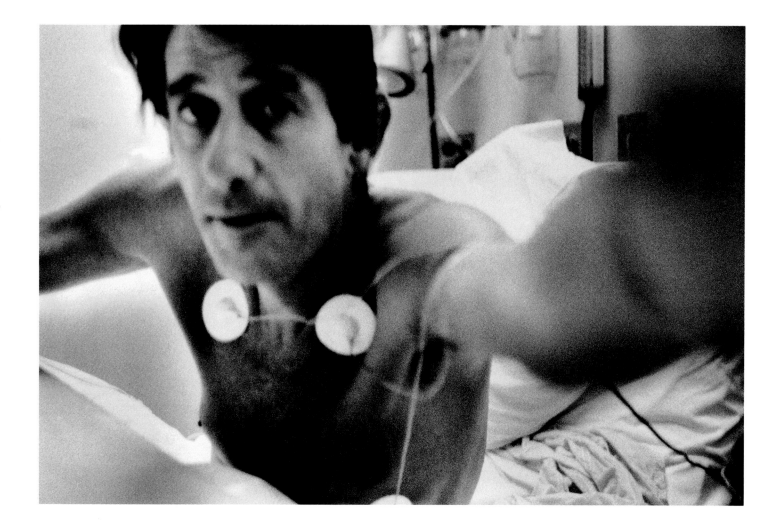

Helmut Newton
SELF-PORTRAIT DURING AN
ELECTROCARDIOGRAM, NEW YORK

Sylvia Plachy
MONKEYS AT A CRACK ADDICTION
RESEARCH LABORATORY

Life's what you make it. My ambition was always just to get married and have a heap of kids, and I did it. I don't want anything more out of life. Let's say you had a nice cupboard or something. That's only material. That doesn't mean as much as somebody really being nice to you. It's no good having a nice shiny house that nobody can come inside, is it?

There used to be 20 kids in my yard every morning, and I had swings and things. They all respect me today, bald and old as they are. And they say, "G'day, Lail, how are you?" There's not one kid today who plays in my yard who doesn't respect me. There's really not much more in life you can have.

I once pulled a man out of a bog, and when I did, he said, "I wish you all the luck in the world." I told him I didn't need any more.

Lailene Middleton,
of Tungamah, Australia, has spent 17 years cooking meals for sheep shearers

If I weren't here, you wouldn't have any reason to be here. One human being is pointless without another. We exist for each other. We're interdependent, emotionally and otherwise. God just put us here to take care of each other. That's how it started; that's how it's always been.

We're not here to work toward a greater goal after this life. The earth started out perfect in the first place. I think the only reason we keep thinking there has to be more is because of our egos. I don't know where egos come from or how we got to the point where we thought people have to achieve. Everything was just fine until we decided we needed to develop the world. The concept that we need to keep evolving and developing and being better and better is what's screwing this whole world up. And, by the way, I don't put anything on my steak either. By that I mean: I'm a simple person with a simple philosophy about the meaning of life.

I just got up. I mean, really, who cares? Let's have a party.

Sue Ellen Radovich
drives a wheat truck and school bus in Holcomb, Kansas

I didn't have a very good time these last 40 years. My husband died so I had to raise the kids. I worked just to provide their food and clothing, and I got nothing out of it, no car, no house.

Still, when everything is O.K., like it is now, I'm happy. I'm glad the revolution happened. I would like people to work hard. If people would work harder, it would make our life better.

I want people to be happy and have good times together. Nothing else. I don't want to be rich, not now. It's too late for that. At home I raise hens and rabbits. I try and get along with everyone. I like to see people coming and going. I smile and try to be pleasant. People usually smile back. That's what's important.

Zdenka Podrouzkova
is a restaurant rest room attendant in Prague, Czechoslovakia

I live where the world ends—the Dead Sea is over there, the road ends here. I don't know why God put me here. It's not a good life. I'm just living. But it's an easy life. As you make your bed, you lie on it. Sometimes we complain. But eventually we realize God intended this life for us and there's nothing we can do about it. God created us in order to judge us. I don't know more to say. My immediate purpose is to go to the celebration of our new kindergarten and see the princess. The princess is coming soon. I'm going to show her how I make butter.

Salma Abu-Quaoud,
a Jordanian Bedouin, spins wool

This week's philosophy—it changes every day sometimes—is that every day without work is a day gained in the bank account of life. Life's meaning starts with the reversal of the theme: work before pleasure. Just enjoy. I'm glad there are serious people. They work hard and probably don't enjoy their lives, but without them the system would fall apart. The beer we drink, the glass we drink from wouldn't be available. At the same time, ignorance is bliss. For some, happiness is family. For others, it comes at five o'clock when the bell goes off to end the day—they don't know what they're missing. I contribute to society by proving it's possible to have a good time. And I'm having a damn good time.

Giles Carlyle-Clarke
is a British sailor, circumnavigator and antiques exporter

William Albert Allard
BASQUE GIRLS

As a six-year-old, I fled through ice and snow with my brothers and sisters, pursued by Red Army soldiers. For much of 1945, it seemed, our young lives hung upon a silken thread. At one point, I remember, my youngest brother's eyes had begun to roll up into his head, as he came close to dying. At another, we sat in a frigid coal ship, set to sail to the West, only to be removed from the boat at the last minute. In time, we managed to escape, and we survived.

Since then I have sailed off the Vietnamese coast, helping save 9,507 boat people. I have been caught in a MiG attack on Eritrea, watching villages strafed with cluster bombs and napalm. I have been part of a team hunted by Soviet troops on the outskirts of Kabul, forced to undertake a long march, over mountains, for 18 hours, before escaping. And at each stage it became clear. Life, life, nothing else but life! Life is the only common bond that humans share, the only thing about which we can all agree. Today we are here to protect life in general: in the tropical rain forests, in the swamps, on the Amazon, on the Rhine. But we are also here to uphold individual life. It is in life that original beauty is contained. I do not mean that beauty comes only from beholding life. I also mean that it is beautiful to feed a hungry child, to dry his tears, to blow his nose. It is beautiful to heal a sick man.

Everything else is ugly.

Rupert Neudeck

is a German journalist who has organized refugee relief efforts in Afghanistan, Cambodia and throughout Africa

Derek Hudson
IRAQI PRISONERS RECEIVING
RATIONS, KUWAIT

Misery, pure misery, hardship and pain, that's been my life, that's all I've known. A poor lad grows up very fast, an orphan even faster. Sometimes I think I was an old man before I was born.

When I was a boy, people said, "When you're born this poor, you'll never know worse," and I believed it. I believed: "There is no dishonor in poverty . . . a poor man is an honest man . . . the poor are generous with the little they have . . . poverty is the best teacher . . . for the man without a house, the world is home . . . suffering builds character . . . the poor are rich in spirit . . . for he who has nothing, everything awaits."

By the time I was 15, I'd suffered so much hardship and need I was assured a future full of freedom, honor, courage, education, hospitality and abundance. My poverty had blessed me with so much good fortune.

I was not naive or stupid. I simply believed all the old sayings. Whoever said "A poor man has nothing to lose" forgot about the limbs. By the time I was 20, I had only one leg. At first, the biggest cruelty was to have been fed so many lies by people I trusted, since nothing they said turned out to be true. It took 30 years to understand that no two lives are alike and one man's truth is another man's lie. Now I remember an old man who used to say "Better to lose a leg than a life" and "He who lives longest suffers most."

I never, never imagined how miserable life could truly be. Things can always get worse, and for me they have.

Adolfo Hernandez

is a bootblack from Santiago, Chile

Patrick Robert
KURDISH REFUGEES
AT THE IRAQI-TURKISH BORDER

LIFE magazine, in a moment of insanity, has asked me to write 250 words on the meaning of life. (I daren't tell them I don't know that many.) *I* am to write about the meaning of life? I, who last night, in the rain, locked the keys in the car and thought *that* was the meaning of life? (Well, it felt like it at the time.)

Life being what it is, I'd say it's occupational therapy twixt life and death. If you don't believe me, try the London Underground's Northern Line during rush hour. It's sort of a do-it-yourself black hole of Calcutta.

I thought I knew all the answers until my six-year-old daughter asked, "Daddy, where does the dark go when you switch on the light?" I told her the dark went to Britain's Labour Party, who hid it.

Come to think of it, my father once said to me: "Life is like a big fish." When I said, "Why is life like a big fish?" he got into a rage and said, "All right, life is *not* like a big fish. Satisfied?"

Recently, I was at one of those Meaning-of-Life parties, and there were many homeopaths in attendance who said a cure for migraines is to stand on one leg in a bowl of custard—provided you wear magenta. A few stiff whiskeys, and I was telling people that life was like a big fish. Among those people I met there was a holy man covered with beads of life and om medallions. "The meaning of life," he began, as he downed a double brandy Alexander. . . . Here he reeled from the room and was sick in the flowerbed. Later on, when he came 'round with his mantra collection box, he sang a loud "om" at me as I dropped in a 50p.

No, folks, there's only one answer to the Mystery of Life. You do as much of it as you can.

Spike Milligan

is considered Britain's clown prince of comedy

If what we know at birth is sabotaged by society, then perhaps it is too late for me to comment on the meaning of life.

Most of us live two lives: one, of private impulses, desires, viciousness and vulnerability; the other, of relative conformity to society.

The quote is from *Spoon River Anthology* and is attributed to Davis Matlock: "Well, I say to live it out like a god, sure of immortal life, though you are in doubt, is the way to live it. If that doesn't make God proud of you then God is nothing but gravitation, or sleep is the golden goal." When I came upon this excerpt, I was taken by its energy. That we are encouraged to accept doubt as incidental. That the concept of God can translate to our own acquisition of self-respect. That our choices (call that morals) guarantee nothing, and yet we are immortal because we demand to be immortal. The arrogance of religions (particularly Western), schools, governments and parents is perhaps the arrogance of answers. Society is by definition the place that teaches people how and why to live. Perhaps its next course will teach eagles to soar.

Sean Penn,

American actor, screenwriter and director, is known for playing brooding outsiders

First off, I don't claim an exclusive inside track on the reason for, or the destiny of, our species. In fact, as an avaricious African American artist— outnumbered, scorned and oppressed— I have never had the opportunity to delve into the meaning of life as a pure philosophical abstraction, notwithstanding that certain rules of thumb help me get out of bed . . . principles that (trying to assert parental prerogative) I have duly passed on to my children.

First and foremost, Ixnay on dreams deferred. Don't take crap! I am not of the IODINE SCHOOL OF THOUGHT: neither secular (i.e., if it hurts it must be good for you and will improve your character) nor religious (i.e., if it hurts on earth you will receive your reward a zillion times over in the hereafter; in fact, I have a pronounced aversion to pain, poverty and unpleasantness).

Second, be gentle, situation permitting ("forgive them, for they know not what they do . . ." etc.). Who knows? Maybe each heart is given the same amount of emotions for a lifetime regardless of the circumstance—so much hate and pity, love and fear per person, issued methodically the way girls used to pass out their kisses before the sexual revolution, and if the heart doesn't have bullets, discrimination or codependency to worry about, it settles for hair dyes and football pools.

I think the old hobo proverb probably got it right: "Try to enjoy the ride, 'cause it's half the trip."

Melvin Van Peebles

is a film and television actor, director, composer, screenwriter and producer

TOP 10 REASONS WE'RE HERE

10. To invent, perfect and mass-produce the Sneaker Phone
9. So dogs and cats don't have to work for a living
8. To tremble at the terrible beauty of the stars, to shed a tear at the perfection of Beethoven's symphonies . . . and to crack a cold one now and then
7. To give the porpoises someone to feel superior to
6. To convert useless oxygen into valuable carbon dioxide
5. To provide cheap entertainment for the Neptunian Telescope People
4. Lather. Rinse. Repeat.
3. To purchase the fine books and magazines of Time Warner, Inc.
2. I think it has something to do with proteins or amino acids or something
1. To *polka*, baby, *polka*

David Letterman

and the *Late Night* writers have extended the boundaries of American TV comedy for a decade

Kevin Horan

BLUEFISH TWO WAYS, NANTUCKET

Ken Heyman
CHILDREN ON A RIDE, 14TH STREET, NEW YORK CITY

David Hiser
AZTEC QUETZAL DANCERS

What is life? It seems that I cannot thoroughly understand it. Whenever I am deep in thought, many things come to mind: my father and his studio, nice colors, the sun, the moon, small hills, flowers and trees, happy little monkeys, birds and all kinds of animals. It is really like an intoxicating paradise to think about their existence. Yet sometimes, when the images blur, I feel perplexed as well. And the only thing I desire is to get back that sense of paradise. The paintbrush and paper help bring the scenery back to me, and I joyfully dissolve in the act of painting. I seem to be close to the forest, mountains, rivers, the changing seasons.

When I am painting, I feel free. I feel I am not following the rules of others. There is no need for me to be labeled a so-called painter before I paint. I just paint because I want to. And I feel grateful that my father shares this view. I guess the sun and moon in his mind are rounder and brighter. This, perhaps, is why he always smiles at the painting paper, why he is always enchanted by mountains, the crowd and flowers. Maybe this is what can be called his love for life. Deep inside, we all cherish love. We harbor happy feelings for little monkeys and other animals. And that is the reason we are here.

Wang Yani,

16, China's most famous child artist, is the youngest person ever honored with a solo exhibition at Washington's Smithsonian Institution

For me, the moment of awakening came just over 70 years ago, when I was 11. It was mid-morning on a Saturday in early April 1920. Free of school, Carl Hammerstrom, a lad who lived up the street, and I crossed the railroad tracks and climbed Swede Hill to explore new terrain.

As we approached the woodlot near the old reservoir, I spotted a bundle of brown feathers clinging to the trunk of a tree. It was a flicker, sleeping, probably tired from migration. But I thought it was dead. Gingerly, I touched it on the back and instantly this inert thing sprang to life, looked at me with wild eyes, then fled on a flash of golden wings. It was like a resurrection: What had seemed dead was very much alive.

Ever since, birds have seemed to me to be the most vivid expression of life. They have dominated my thoughts and my reading, inevitably pulling me into the wider vistas of the environment, including the butterflies, the plants and the rest of the natural world.

The meaning of life? What ignited the life force in the beginning? Certainly not a manlike being up there in the stratosphere. Our kind, Homo sapiens, the dominant primate, has the whip hand, but need we be so egocentric as to think only of ourselves and dismiss the countless other forms of life?

Having nearly drowned last summer, I have become ever more sensitive to the nuances of all living things.

Roger Tory Peterson

is America's leading ornithologist

Teiji Saga
A SNOWDRIFT OF SWANS,
HOKKAIDO ISLAND, JAPAN

Henri Cartier-Bresson
FROM ONE MOMENT TO THE NEXT,
FROM ONE PLACE TO ANOTHER, ANY
OTHER QUESTION WOULD BE FUTILE

Walking along the seashore and looking into the distance where the blue of the water melts into the blue of the firmament, seeing the scum of a single tide on one tiny stretch of beach, I no longer know what meaning is; I no longer know what is meaningful. The colorful striped shells, beautiful and symmetrical, the little fish that shine like silver, twitching imploringly in the scorching sand, unable to bring themselves back to life, the empty crab shells with their bizarre architecture—each is an unimportant entity in nature's wide domain. As a human being, am I indeed more privileged than they are? Do I amount to anything more than a passing pulsebeat in the grand metabolism of living things? If no single being holds significance in all of nature's household, then what really matters after all?

Strange. Having endured this tormenting meditation, I am suddenly liberated upon realizing it is already 11 o'clock. At 11:20 I shall again see the one whom I love most. She has waited for me as I have been waiting for her, for days. Everything that concerns her has absolute meaning to me. Oh, soon we will fall into each other's arms, only to be embraced by a chain of amber, a bracelet of coral. There will be no such thing as death any longer, only a net of meaning spread across our love.

Not so strange. Recently I observed a female macaque monkey and her newborn. Two siblings squatted nearby and carefully observed the little one's every move. With curiosity in its wide eyes, the small creature leaned its outsize head forward so that it seemed on the verge of tipping over. The mother held out her hand protectively. She did not hinder the newborn's movements; instead, she provided an almost imperceptible veil of safety.

The hands that we put around each other in love and the invisible hand that protects all lovers: In their grasp lies all the meaning that this life can bear.

Eugen Drewermann
is a German psychoanalyst and a radical Catholic theologian

On the night of June 3, 1989, I was content. I was in love. I had passed exams for a prestigious job. And I was sitting in my college dorm, working on the final draft of my thesis. Up until that night, I had never bothered to think what I was living for.

Suddenly I heard gunshots. I exited the college gate and encountered horrified people saying that martial law troops had opened fire on civilians and were about to take over Tiananmen Square. My first reaction was to warn my boyfriend. I got on my bike and pedaled along Chang'an Avenue toward the square. I was not sure I could spot him among the crowds. Still, I pedaled. I could not curb the urge in my heart.

I did not find him. Instead, I met the troops at Liubukou, where, I later learned, large numbers of people would be killed that evening. I saw flaming roadblocks adding streaks of red to the dark blue sky. I saw soldiers on foot and in armored personnel carriers, shooting as they advanced. I joined a group retreating into a narrow alley as soldiers chased after us 10 yards back. I heard a bullet go *crack* right next to me. I looked up, only to see blood trickling from a black hole in the back of a young man who still kept running.

I felt as if I were in a dream, unable to feel frightened or to cry. I ran alongside the others, almost mechanically, thinking: I shall not die, my boyfriend shall not die.

When I arrived back at my dorm in the early morning, I couldn't sleep. I waited all day. And then, that evening, he came to take me to his apartment. As I saw him, tears filled my eyes. They were tears for the dead, but, moreover, they were tears for my love, a love so strong it had protected us from death. Suddenly, I realized it was for this love that I had always been living.

We got married soon thereafter. Because of his involvement in the demonstrations, my husband's work was suspended during the purge that followed the crackdown. I have been reassigned to a less important government agency job. But depressing as life has been, our love has never left us. In fact, that love has sustained us, sustained us happily. Even now, though we cannot do much to change our lives, we are confident about the future. There is no difficulty our love cannot overcome since ours is a love capable of defying even death.

Ding Lili
(not her real name) is a translator in Beijing

Unrequited love is the meaning of life. We're here to love but not to be loved, to give but not receive. Our mission in this world is to improve humanity and leave a better history than we found. Only selfless love has such power. Only love without interest or expectation of reward can change human beings.

I believe in reincarnation. Each time we return in a more degraded form, and our suffering increases. Each time we are called upon to give more and get less. That is how we must evolve until our sense of giving is stronger than our sense of greed.

It's easy to love when the feeling is returned. To love and be loved is an enchantment, a pleasure, a delight. But that kind of love doesn't change anything; it doesn't advance us as human beings. It simply pleases the pair involved. It is a limited love.

To give love without receiving love is the truest love and brings the greatest happiness there is in life. But what happens is our sense of giving is far less developed than our inclination to be greedy. So when we love someone and it's not returned, we stop loving them. When we do that, we negate ourselves and our capacity to be a good human being. To make a better world we must love each other more. If we insist they love us back before we love them first, we make a stand-off no one can break.

Adolfo Barcella
is a hotel concierge in Buenos Aires, Argentina

Lori Grinker
DEBUTANTES, BUCKHEAD, GEORGIA

Bill Eppridge
FOOTBALL FANS, ALABAMA

Most people believe in God. They are searching for the meaning of life. But humanity must die one day; each of us is fragile and delicate.

Many people are immobile. They live in confusion, yearning for something or someone. They lead difficult lives. In facing crises, they find a fierce light.

Let us weep for the disabled. They are becoming more visible to us. Let us exult. Let us help one another.

The theater has held the meaning of my life. My life has been the theater. I now work, challenged by aphasia—and I will focus most of my future work on disability.

Good music is magnificent: vibrating, rhythmic, melodic, harmonic.

Comedy is good for breaking open the mind.

Look at the sky. Infinite planets and stars. Galaxies unseen and unimagined.

Joseph Chaikin
is a theatrical actor, director and writer

TIME/LIFE

There was a time in your life
When you were neither seen nor heard
Except by those who have eyes and ears

Then there is a time in your life
When you are seen and heard
Except by those who have no eyes and
*   no ears*

Then there comes a time in your life
When you are not seen or heard Again?
Except by those who have eyes and ears

These, then, are matters of the heart

Abdullah Ibrahim
is a Cape Town–born pianist and composer who recorded the first South African jazz album

The majority of people respond to the question, "Is life fair?" with a resounding "No!" Through my exposure to treating people with life-threatening illnesses, I have come to realize that we must use our pain in constructive ways if we are to make life meaningful.

Recently, I reread an old myth. It concerned a child who was willing to sacrifice himself to conserve the life of his king and country. He convinced his parents to consent to his act and, as he was about to be sacrificed to the demon, he laughed joyously. In response, those witnessing the sacrifice stopped and assumed an attitude of prayer. I believe that when you know why the boy laughed, you know the meaning of life.

The Bible tells us that the Son of Man came not to be served but to serve and to ransom his life for the good of the many. The boy knew he was achieving immortality in the only way possible—through love, in his case an unconditional love that expressed itself in sacrifice for the good of many others. In his short life, he was doing all that anyone could hope to do. That realization brought him true joy. He was also laughing at the attachment the others had to their bodies, something he has transcended.

"The best part of a good man stays," said William Saroyan. "It stays forever. Love is immortal and makes all things immortal." He may just as well have been talking about the boy. So, too, George Bernard Shaw when he said: "This is the true joy in life, the being used for a purpose recognized by yourself as a mighty one; the being thoroughly worn out before you are thrown on the scrap heap; the being a force of Nature instead of a feverish selfish little clod of ailments and grievances complaining that the world will not devote itself to making you happy."

As the poet said: Life is no brief candle, but a torch to be held high before passing it along to future generations. I believe we are all here to be bright torches that light one another's way. We are here to use our lives and burn up—not burn out. We must find our own particular way of loving the world and put our energy into it. Decide your way of loving and you will be rewarded.

Bernie Siegel,
surgeon, runs self-healing cancer support groups and is the author of *Love, Medicine and Miracles*

Sometimes I see the hidden life of people: the lives behind them, before them, the bad events, illnesses, crises, weak points, passages. I see it in their hands. I feel it from them.

We have to be aware of everything around us: the weather, the time, body chemistry and the unknown things such as astrology and the supernatural. Life is so mysterious. People are in misery, and they don't know how to get out, get help or free themselves. Life is total freedom, but we're trapped in our own civilization, culture, religion, teachings. We're equipped with fear, ignorance, unhappiness. Desire is the big evil, the big temptation. Many people carry on in life without knowing this. We do so much for our bodies but not for our souls.

Pay attention to yourself, monitor your thinking and capture the villains within. Know what it is in you that would make people suffer more, make people suffer less. Know this and you know how to use your thinking and abilities to bring peace. Certain people have certain duties, a talent. The meaning of life is to see this mission, fulfill it and make the maximum use of your life for your benefit and mankind's.

Kanda Anuman Rajadhon,
homemaker, filmmaker and palm reader, lives in Bangkok, Thailand

We could take the road of negativity. We could deny everything, not believe in anything, simply live a life, love for love's sake, art for art's sake, life for life's sake only, without any other meaning. But it's like you're fighting something. You need to keep going in your life. You need to keep *one* sense in your life, lay a foundation, live in accordance with a set of principles and beliefs.

Felipe Sagardia
is a Basque shepherd from Pamplona, Spain

As a banker's daughter, I found that religion meant little to me until I married a Buddhist priest. Even then, through the first 10 years of married life, I found myself too busy being wife and mother to devote much time to the teachings of the Buddha. Then, 10 years ago, quite suddenly, something happened. A moment of truth. It hit me like a lightning bolt. I was on a visit to a small Buddhist temple. After a sleepless night, I found myself overwhelmed with a revelation so powerful that I felt electrified. I had realized, at precisely three a.m. in the dead of a February night, that the surest eventuality in life is death. I understood that no matter what your station—carpenter, lawyer, government official—you always have to do your best in whatever work comes your way. Only then can you express your gratitude for having been endowed with life. Only then can you rest assured of reaching paradise after death.

Ayano Otani

is deputy chief of a Buddhist ossuary in Kyoto, where the ashes of 18,000 dead are preserved

We read the coca leaves to understand life. Whatever you want to know can be learned from the leaves because they contain all knowledge. Coca tells the truth.

Coca leaves have divine power because God chewed them and was forever pleased. A million years later, when His son was crucified and in terrible pain, God cured the wounds by chewing coca leaves to make a salve. So Coca is loved even by our Lord.

To find the meaning of life, we must look to Coca for advice. If we ignore its advice, we damn ourselves and deserve what we get. Coca reveals all—if someone is dead or alive, sick or happy, frightened or sad. Coca will answer whatever you ask. Nothing can hide from the eyes of Coca. Spirits, souls, devils and dreams, all can be seen. Coca tells the truth.

Raymundo Marca

is a healer and diviner of coca leaves in La Paz, Bolivia

It once happened that I had stones in the kidney. I was in severe, unbearable pain. I started asking God for help because I couldn't stand the idea of surgery. Then, suddenly, the stones dissolved completely, as if a stone destroyer, using sound waves, had simply turned the mass into gravel so that it could pass through my urinary tract. On other occasions I have had simple dreams that, two days later, came true, as if I had looked through the diary of God. When you desire something severely, it becomes "embodied." Many, many events have convinced me that things are predestined, that there is a design for everything.

Often, it is through suffering that we acquire knowledge. Just as we gain immunity through disease, just as good springs from evil (the biggest contributions in science occur during periods of war), just as the earth releases pent-up pressure through volcanoes and earthquakes, through suffering we find the time to think and meditate and, in turn, find wisdom. Even the cumulative result of failure opens one's internal eye.

At first glance, life appears meaningless, futile, full of contradictions and absurdities. But a deeper, meditating look uncovers beauty, order and harmony, revealing life as a supreme accomplishment of eternal wisdom. From the atom to the galaxy, a master design is at work and at play, created by a master builder unequaled in his attributes and grace. All of creation is an act of love and providence, a drama imbued with meaning: the flower sprouting from the bud, the child emerging from the womb, the human race evolving from the furthest branch of the tree of existence. When we discover that there are tens of thousands of species of botanic life, when we are stunned by the variations of human DNA, fingerprints and lip prints—we understand that this infinite variation is deliberate, created by a superior will, a superior ego. This realization is not a thought or a theory; it is a feeling, a sense, in one's heart, of the presence of God.

The march of life from bacterium to Shakespeare, from bushman to the Prophet, has been a steady advance. We have a natural inclination to walk in step with this march, i.e., to improve ourselves and upgrade our standards as we open the sleeping flower within us. This is actually the essence of all religions. In simple words: Life is a mission of awareness and awakening and deep enlightenment. We are here to sense this divine presence beyond all phenomena. We are here to recognize a deep urge in our hearts to act in harmony, in conformity and in love with these divinities.

Mustapha Mahmoud,

Egyptian physician and Islamic scholar, is the author of God and Man

I believe that being true to the self is most important in life—to have a free heart, a pure soul and a pure mind. We all live, or should live, for the fulfillment of the self. We are all mirror images of each other; whatever we feel in ourselves we feel in others. I believe that we create our own lives.

The changes, the choices, the paths, the characters, it is all up to you how you want this play called "life" to go.

We always choose paths according to the need of experience and according to how we really know ourselves.

One challenge of our adventure on earth is to rise above dead systems—wars, manipulations, destruction—to refuse to be a part of them, and instead to be a peace warrior, a love warrior and express the highest selves we know how to be. Not to judge, but to love unconditionally and respect each other.

Intuition should play the main role in everything we do. Through the creative source of the mind and the unlimited power of the spirit all our deepest wishes come true. For me the meaning is that we are all one, and the only true reality is the spirit. Believing in the power of spirit is simply to have a passion for life, to learn, to grow, to evolve and most of all to love, and live each day and each moment of the day to the fullest.

Tatjana Patitz,

model and actress, was raised in Sweden

"The meaning of life is to see," said Hui-nêng, the seventh century Chinese sage. Indeed, the cow can look at me, but I can *see* the cow—a living being. We have become addicted to looking-at: We look-at the world through telescopes, microscopes, TV tubes. The more we look-at it, the less we *see*. If we could still *see* the corpses, the starving babies on the screen, we would weep, pray. Where seeing is demeaned to looking-at, life seems meaningless.

For me, drawing is seeing intensified until the seeing and the drawing fuse into the single act of seeing-drawing and the meaning of life discloses itself in landscape, plant, human face. I discovered seeing-drawing in Africa when serving as a doctor in Albert Schweitzer's Lambaréné hospital. I did not want to look-at Africa and Africans, so I drew to *see* them clearly. They became part of me. When I drew the Grand Docteur, he spoke of what motivated him: "Reverence for life is the only sound basis for a viable ethics." He did not look-at the joys and pains around him. He *saw*. This same reverence I detected in Pope John XXIII. While drawing him and his Vatican council, I saw him meeting the mighty and the powerless. He was all eye. He took in each one so totally that he forgot he was a pope.

The doctor-in-me has written about "being human against all odds." The odds are formidable. I believe that the oldest part of our brain is what a lizard's was 250 million years ago, and it still functions as such. Meanwhile, the mammalian and the human brain have enveloped it, and only its latest outcropping, the prefrontal cortex, has empowered us to be aware of our own life and, by extension, that of others. Empathy and compassion are truly new phenomena.

The reptile in us still looks-at and craves. The human can see. The artist-within-me draws, sees the meaning manifested in all that lives, as neither reading nor thinking could yield. Hui-nêng's *seeing* fuses with the Protestant doctor's and the Catholic pope's reverence to celebrate the meaning of life.

Frederick Franck,
Netherlands-born artist and dental surgeon, is the author of *The Zen of Seeing*

David Hockney
FREDDA BRINGING ANN AND ME A CUP OF TEA, APRIL 16, 1983, LOS ANGELES

Who is bought and sold?
Who is beyond the law?
Whose body is a battleground?
Who is free to choose?
Who knows that empathy can change the world?
Who is healed? Who is housed?
Whose fictions become history?
Who does the crime? Who does the time?
Who salutes longest? Who prays loudest?
Who dies first? Who laughs last?

Barbara Kruger,
American artist, combines images and texts to make political statements

David Heiden
ETHIOPIAN REFUGEES
AT THE SUDANESE BORDER

I feel we're lost. I can't explain it. *Maybe we'll go to Manila, but I don't know which way to go. Two bridges are out, the rivers are flooding. The flashes keep alternating white and red.* I think I'm closer to God now. What can you do but laugh it off? I'm not afraid, but my wife is. I have my children and not much more. Material things aren't very important right now. My life is following the footprints in the sand. I think I've led a good life. I'm sure of it. I actually feel it. The sand, the ash, also fulfill the words of God. You'll never appreciate God without natural disasters. It's only now I see I am meaningless. I can't even compare myself to a microbe. I'm naked, bare, nothing. I can't control the situation. Not even the wisest of men can control this volcano and this typhoon. Nature has meaning and nature is God. *The leaves are too heavy. The tree limbs are breaking from the weight of the ash and are falling on the road.* God controls the universe. Who created this ash? Even astronauts, after flying to the moon, started believing in God. We're here to prove the existence of God. If we mean nothing, how do we prove the existence of God? By accepting in our hearts we're nothing, we prove His existence. On this earth we should live upright, be tremendous lovers—first to God, then everything else follows. . . . I'm a wandering lamb now. I don't even know where to get my next drink. My house was flooding just a few hours ago. It may have been taken away by now. I'll accept it. If the mud and waters come flowing toward me, I'll accept death. Why not? Nothing else matters. Not bed sheets . . . *Listen to that roar.*

Loy Parass,

a dentist from the Philippines, has been made homeless by the eruption of Mount Pinatubo, among the century's most destructive volcanoes

W here can you draw the line between your life and the next person's life? How good can your life be if the next person's life is rotten?

Life in Guatemala is worth nothing. In a war that has spanned three decades, 100,000 have died, 40,000 have disappeared. You can have someone killed for a bottle of whiskey. My husband and I had a theater group. We were very critical of the poverty, the army, the privileged few. Somebody shot at the side of our car. People followed us. My husband received a letter saying he was going to be killed. We had to escape in a hurry, leaving everything, just like that. In Guatemala you can keep your life if you close your mouth and don't rock the boat. The meaning of life is to keep living— despite people shooting at you, despite a cholera epidemic—so you can make life better.

Margarita Kenetic

is a Guatemalan actress, playwright and political activist

I was forced to leave my home as a young man and sacrifice everything for that horrible life as a soldier in the bush. The worst thing that happened to me was when I was caught in an ambush by Rhodesian forces. The situation made me wonder a lot about the creator, about why he would cause such suffering, why he could allow me to be healthy one moment and in a near-death state the next. But since then I've realized that war and suffering are unnatural, brought about by man and by greed.

The situation in Zimbabwe is quite pleasing now. There is no more fighting, no racial and tribal discrimination. Lives were lost for the right cause: to liberate everybody regardless of race, color or tribe, to allow each individual to sustain himself and his family with a job and a little bit of land. Having these things, without suffering, is the purpose of life. This makes life meaningful. This is the highest purpose: to be able to live a reasonable life.

Jabulani Moyo,

conservationist from the village of Marinoha in Matabeleland, Zimbabwe, was a medic in the Rhodesian civil war

B efore I left my family, they all sat at the table and we made a small party. We had salad, rice, a little meat, some cheese and olives. My mother had been preparing for this for a long time. All my family was there, 15 or 20 people. Each one took the microphone and told impressions about my family and about me. Everybody but my sister. She was crying so hard. I haven't listened to the tape yet. It's too painful. It's the first time I have been away from home.

I can't explain what's on my heart. Family is very important to me. I feel that mine is living through a very difficult moment. My father is retired, my mother works many nights. I sold our television to pay for my ticket to the West. Now my family is without a son and a television. It's just a television, black-and-white, but it's very important. It is the only distraction, our small window on the West.

The meaning of life is not to be in trouble with the police. The meaning of life is that a person can study, work, create a family and live "the right life." By this, I mean enjoying the good things and not being involved in drug trafficking or crime. I believe in God. But until this moment I have never been in a church. I can go now, but I don't know what to do. Thirty years without church is a long time. The Albanian people have lived only with danger and despair. Still, I believe. We are the sons of God, and we should do His work. We have a duty to help others, to help poor people. We have to create possibilities for them. If you have no possibilities, you cannot live.

Ilir Tivari,

Albanian refugee from Tirana, is presently stationed at a transit camp near Vienna, Austria

I asked some guys in the lounge car of the train I was riding along the Mississippi what they thought the meaning of life was.

"Life was intended to be an experiment," says Bill, who has had the most to drink. "Not in the scientific manner and not in the biblical manner, but of the two."

"Oh, hell," says Larry. "There's no meaning. We're just lucky to be here. We're just growing on earth like a fungus. A goddamn happy little fungus."

"I am not a fungus, Larry," says Bill.

A man with long blond hair named Turtle leans in. "It's to learn how to evolve through cycles to a higher plane and go to another planet."

"Venus," says Bill. "I would choose Venus."

"Also," says Turtle, "it's to evolve into a much better head space."

Larry points at Bill. "By God, he's tryin'." Bill raises his glass. A camp counselor named Joe says, "Life is like a river, but it all depends on who is looking at the river."

"Christ Jesus," says Larry, and he rubs his face. Through the window we watch the Mississippi and are quiet for a moment.

"I have been observant of every species," says Bill. "And I have a degree in sociology so I know of these things. I will tell you the meaning. . . ."

"Uh-oh," says Larry. "Here it comes." But Bill's number comes over the speaker for dinner, and he gets up. "Aw, Bill!" says Larry. "The suspense is going to kill us!"

"I shall return," says Bill, but my stop comes before he does.

"Well, here's to you, Red," Larry toasts me as I gather my things. "Oh, and I was just kidding about the 'no meaning' part. I just like giving you all a hard time."

Lynda Barry
is a cartoonist and humorist

Bob Adelman
ON THE 37TH DAY, HE RESTED

W e are here to attempt to give more to this life than we take from it, a task that, if undertaken properly, is impossible. The more we give, the more we get. But that's the point.

We are here to discover, develop and cultivate, in loving stewardship of our world, our neighbors and ourselves. Each of us is intended to grow and flourish within the power of our talents on every dimension of worldly existence: the Intellectual, the Aesthetic and the Moral—the great *I AM*— in such a way as to find our place in the overarching realm of the Spiritual, the ultimate context of it all.

There is more to life than meets the eye. Much is required. But more is offered. We are participants in a grand enterprise, not called upon to consume with endless desire, but rather to care and create in such a way as to free the spirit of this vast creation to love and glorify its creator forever.

Why? Because it's good. And that's good enough for me.

Thomas Morris,
philosopher, teaches courses on the meaning of life at the University of Notre Dame

Nan Goldin
SHARON NURSING COOKIE TWO MONTHS
BEFORE SHE DIED, PROVINCETOWN

(Overleaf)
Martine Barrat
HARLEM BLOCK PARTY

John Bryson
COUNTRYSIDE, BÜRGENSTOCK, SWITZERLAND

I took an old piece of barren soil some years back, and with my mulches and yard clippings and things, I actually watched that plot grow back to six inches of topsoil. It took me three years to restore the earth organically. You could reach in just like reaching your hand into coffee grounds. And it was alive.

I was growing squash on that plot. One day I went and got my little boys, who were playing in their sandbox, and I said, "Boys, sit on this log with me," and we set there and I spread the squash leaves and it was like looking through the canopy of a tropical forest. The squashes were big and my boys was little and they were looking at the little cosmos I had grown there about 10 feet square. We could see insects a-buzzing and a-flying: the plant eaters and the predatory insects. I said to my sons, "I wouldn't spray that for ten million dollars. All the natural processes of life are happening right there." And they looked in amazement.

That's life to me, that whole scene there. We are all in under this canopy. We ain't outside of this thing. As humans, we are the shepherds, the caretakers. We have enormous power, and that's what we're here for: to use that power properly, to walk softly upon the earth, under this canopy of life. My dad always told me: Walk softly. Use this and use that, but restore this and restore that. This is the brilliance that's given to man.

Bob Ferguson,

country music songwriter and television producer, is an organic farming advocate who works for the Mississippi Band of Choctaws

Michael Melford
MAPLE TREE

Neal Slavin
PRIEST, FÁTIMA, PORTUGAL

When I was 20, my parents died. I didn't know how to do anything, so I came here. I make tea for people who pass by. I was married, but my wife died five years ago. We never had children. We never knew why. When I was young, I wanted to be happy, walk with my friends and have fun. Now, I don't think of life as a day-by-day or moment-by-moment thing. I think only of the afterlife. I'm just in agony with what I'm doing now, and all I can think of is when God will take my life away. I make enough each day to get cigarettes and some bread. This is my luck. Life has become complex. People are so busy working to support their families, they don't have time to come here anymore to remember their dead families.

My life has no meaning. I don't know how to read. I don't even have the mind to think, to give meaning to my life. I've been here too long. If I had known this is how it would be, I'd have learned a profession. If I had known I'd lead a miserable life, I'd have made something out of myself.

We don't live for anything. We live for ourselves. Nobody helps another. Your own won't even help you. It's your own power in God that gets you help. People were invented to live, to work, to have a bad life.

Mustafa Ibrahim
lives by the roadside in Cairo's City of the Dead, where he has sold hot tea for 35 years

Life has no meaning. Life's purpose is to suffer for the sins we've committed. All my life I have suffered. If we have committed sins in our last life, we have to suffer in this life. Though I really don't know what sins I've committed, I am here to pray for deliverance from my sins.

Panchi Bor,
a Bengali woman spurned by her family, awaits death in a prayer hall in northern India

I am a thousand miles from my home. Faraway working, trying to live, to maintain a family. I miss them so much every day. I can't read or write, but still I am here trying to write them a postcard. This all makes me very sad. Life is very hard. One has to struggle to live.

God has put us here to work and to atone, to work and to pay. I pay by working so far from home. There is nothing I would rather do than be near my family all the time. But if I want to live well without knowing how to read or write, I have to work far from home. I have to pay so that one day things might go better for us.

We pay in this life by working, forcing ourselves through life—and suffering. We live to pay and we pay through suffering.

Cesar Rodriguez,
railroad gandy dancer from Fort Worth, Texas, repairs train tracks in Wyoming

I live on the other side of the mirror, where "respectable" people cast out the parts of themselves they don't want to see. That makes me an outcast, just like Jesus. I think most people are ashamed of themselves so they pretend to be different than they really are. The person they pretend to be, of course, is always worse than the one they are. I see it every day. A man thinks one thing, says another, feels a third, then acts entirely differently. They come to me so they can just be who they are, unload themselves, drop the respectable act. They have to, otherwise they'll explode where their wives or bankers or generals might see.

In this world, money is all that matters. With enough money, a murderer is called a saint. The rich buy the truths that suit them each season, as if truths were fashions from Paris and Rome.

Angelina Santamaria
is a Buenos Aires prostitute

My life means nothing now. I have no reason to live. It's seven months since my husband died, and each second has been a century. There is only the agony of his absence, and that will never end. Nothing gives me comfort, nothing stops the pain—not my children or their children, not the church, not the Scriptures, not the sun, not the rain, not the past, not the future. There is only pain.

I know this is not right. The priest tells me and I hear his words, but they mean nothing. My children are hurt because they think I should want to continue for their sake, or for their children's. But they don't really need me, and they don't stop the pain.

It would be easier to be empty than to carry the memory of 40 years of a magical love. We lived for each other from the first day we met. Our love was the kind you found in the old movies or the legends or the songs. I was 14 when we met, and it was love at first sight. He was kind and pure and gentle and good. He was brilliant and loving and bubbling with life. And he was so handsome, so very, very handsome. He knew my every thought, and I knew his. He even knew my dreams. Our romance never ended. It still hasn't. I am as in love as I ever was, except now he is dead.

Friends say, "My God, you should be grateful for so many years." But since I was 14, he's been in every memory, in every thought. I can't walk down the street without remembering our steps. I can't look at my children without seeing his face. I can't cook a meal without seasoning it to his taste. Everything I know, everything I remember since I was a child now haunts me with his death.

Why wasn't I the one who died?

Mercedes Loyola
is a retired teacher in Santiago, Chile

When I was a teenager, our family was poor and hungry. In the evening, our parents sent us out because the Mau Mau would come to recruit young boys to join them in the forest. During the day, we were subjected to the Colonial Home Guard, who would round us up to check if we had been in contact with the Mau Mau. In the night, we feared the Mau Mau, in the day, the Home Guards. Young people had lost all purpose for living, and desperation set in.

One day the Home Guards came to my village and took all the boys to jail. They marched us into the forest to collect firewood. Since I was the youngest and smallest, I was unable to carry much or to walk as fast, so a guard beat me. He hurt me so bad I had scars for many years.

Later in life I became headmaster of a primary school. A middle-aged man came to place his child in one of my classes, but I realized I had no room at all. I looked at this man and immediately knew. This was the guard who had beaten me nine years before.

A spirit caught me. I understood that I had to find space for his boy. I could not repeat the harm that had been done to me. I asked him, "Do you know me?" He said, "No." I asked him if he remembered a night in July of 1956. Just then, the man looked at my face and started crying. He began to walk away, but I stopped him, saying, "Wait. I'll take the child. I have carried scars for years, but I have forgiven you all those things." That man might have left me permanently disabled, but in allowing me to help his boy, he made me feel fulfilled in what I wanted to do for young people. Fulfillment in life comes from giving your whole life to others. The meaning of life is to serve those who are suffering.

Joel Kinagwi,
from the village of Menga in central Kenya, is the general secretary of the Africa Alliance of YMCAs

What a preposterous question! Like being punched in the face. The essential truth about the existence of man is in the Gospels. What we are, what we hope, what we need, is contained in the Gospels. But they can be difficult. An easier bridge to their meaning is Saint Francis of Assisi.

Simply, Saint Francis says the key to the purpose of life is giving. In giving, you find happiness. You find peace. If you give, you find you are serving your purpose in life. In loving, you find love.

Franco Zeffirelli
is an Italian film and stage director

I believe that every single event in life happens as an opportunity to choose love over fear. Everything good in my life has resulted from having chosen love, by which I mean joy, hope and acceptance of the spiritual quest we are born with. Under the heading fear comes the feeling that we're not good enough, not deserving enough; society tells you that fulfillment comes from gaining material goods. But something deep inside you recognizes that there's got to be more to life. And that longing is the longing to love yourself.

I was doing a show on victims confronting their criminals. A 17-year-old girl was on the air speaking to the man who, four years earlier, had beaten her beyond recognition and left her for dead. She'd had 17 surgeries and complete facial reconstruction. She said to him, "I don't hate you. I hate what you did to me. And I have had to learn to forgive you so I could go on with my own life." To this day it is the most powerful thing I've ever seen. In that moment, she expressed why we're here—to learn to love in spite of the human condition, to transcend the human condition of being fearful. We get so bogged down in worldly things we don't understand that we're here for a spiritual quest. Understanding that this journey is the most exciting part of being human has revolutionized my life.

Oprah Winfrey,
talk show host, is the diva of daytime television

I was always a really happy person. The worst thing that ever happened to me was that I didn't get the house cleaned up or I didn't have quite enough money to pay the electric bill. You always worry. But when something really tragic happens to you, you start wondering, "Why was I put here?"

My son is a very nice person. If you talked to him, you would not believe that he is in prison for 50 years for a crime he didn't commit. When something like that happens, it changes your whole outlook. It completely destroys everything that was ever important to you. I have thought, "God, just let me die. I cannot handle the pain of this." You can't die, but you want to die. Then I thought, "If I die, what would happen to my son?"

It used to be extremely important to me for my hair and makeup to be perfect. Nothing is important now except him. The only reason I work is so I can send him money. The only reason I breathe is so I can take care of him. I live for him. Even if he was guilty, I still would have loved him and taken care of him, but it would not have destroyed me this way.

I don't have a chair in my apartment. I don't have a couch. I have a bed and a TV, and that's it. All my money has gone to pay his legal expenses. We've paid $68,000, and I don't even care. I can sit on the floor, sit on the bed. That's just fine because he might need something. After what I've been through, I can't imagine why you would be here only to take care of yourself. I think we're here to take care of someone else.

Nelda Jo Powell
is a waitress in Oklahoma City, Oklahoma

Steve McCurry
REVEREND PHILIP CHANEY
AT SUMTER COUNTY JAIL, FLORIDA

Angela Fisher
STICK FIGHT COMPETITION AMONG
SURMA TRIBESMEN, ETHIOPIA

W
ho knows why we're here? No
one knows. You can say you do, but
you can't. All you can say is what I said. It
ain't over 'til it's over. And that's all.

Yogi Berra,
former major league catcher and
manager, is the sage of baseball

Tomas Muscionico
HEMINGWAY LOOK-ALIKE FESTIVAL,
KEY WEST, FLORIDA

Dan Higgins
ORLANDO, FLORIDA

Life is an insane barrage of random madness and confusion, mixed with streams and semistreams of order and happiness. It's like a giant, bizarre cake made of gunpowder and sugar. Unlike a real cake with a real recipe, its ratio of ingredients can change constantly, making it almost impossible to accurately describe the taste at any instant.

Personally, I think the reason we are here is that it was too crowded where we were supposed to go.

Life is like going on a ride. Sharing the ride with the people we care about won't necessarily lessen the insanity but may make it a lot easier to deal with (if it is negative) and a lot more enjoyable (if it is positive).

If it rains today, fine. I love to watch the rain.

Steven Wright,
comedian, is the duke of deadpan

We are here to find more golf balls than we lose.

Jim Gaines
is the managing editor and publisher of LIFE magazine

Enrico Ferorelli
STUDIO 54, NEW YORK CITY

1975

1980

1983

1991

1988

Nicholas Nixon
THE BROWN SISTERS, 1975-1991

"Who am I?" is the primordial question to which introspection answers, "I am a particle of this live organism called the earth." The Planet Earth is a sentient being that thinks, speaks, feels, breathes and has a soul, just like a man does. The Incan priest, or *altomisayo,* speaks with the living earth as he speaks with the stars and with the wind and with the sky. He performs rituals that let man experience his natural unity with the universe, what we call the great cosmic egg, or *teximuyo.*

Life is because life must be. At first, life doesn't know it exists. It lacks form, number or geometry. It is unaware of itself. This ignorance, prior to consciousness, compels life to seek itself. Thus, it unites itself, this unity providing form. The instant life takes shape, it separates into contrasting forms, like night and day, so as to be aware of itself. That is the nature of life, duality conceived from unity. An embryo is engendered by the union of two separate beings. As a fetus in the womb it enjoys pure happiness and oneness but remains unaware: To become conscious, it must separate, be born, becoming totally other.

Life and death are cosmic breath. To live and to die is to breathe, to inhale and exhale, inhale and exhale. People speak of another life, but there is only one. In it you have many human forms. Each person designs his own destiny. Right now you are designing how you will live in the future, where you will live, the physical body you will take, the family of your birth and the one you will engender. When there is nothing more for you to learn from human form, you will take another. The purpose of life is to continue developing consciousness.

Freddy Arévalo,
an environmental engineer and Incan priest, lives near Lake Titicaca in the Andes

Frans Lanting
SCATTERING CLOUDS OF A STORM FRONT DRIFT ACROSS THE INDIAN OCEAN

We often think we know what is good for us. We want a promotion, for example; we get it. But it does not prove to be a blessing. In my friend's case—a top guy in the army—obtaining his new post meant a transfer to the battlefront, where he lost his life. I know how much his parents regretted the long longed-for promotion. Apparent misfortune, in a similar twist, may turn out to be a blessing. In one popular Indian folk tale, a prince had cut his finger and his minister told him it was all for the good. The minister was promptly imprisoned for his heartlessness. But that very evening the prince, who was about to be offered in sacrifice by the tribesmen of the forest, was suddenly set free because they determined his body was not "whole."

The only way to judge an event in life is to look at it from high enough, to see it in the order and dimension of the timeless. When we see pain, suffering and inequalities, we don't understand or we jump to false conclusions. We see only the broken arc of a complete circle.

Instead, life is a field for progress and progressive harmony. Each one of us has a part to play which he alone can execute. This role, based on our real nature—what Hindu scriptures call *svabhāva*—can be discovered. An individual's aim in life must be to find out the "law of his being" and act according to his *svadharma.*

This discovery is no easy task. Normally, we are aware of our ego, the surface self that is a bundle of contradictory impulses. But we can find the true self, our best self, by a process of standing back and surveying our needs. Abandoning desire and self-assertion, accepting the challenges of life in a state of stable, unwavering peace will result in this supreme revelation. When life's shocks turn our eyes inward, we rise above contingencies of time and place. Our perspective changes. The greatest of sorrows is transformed into a luminous vibration. We see into the life of things. Life itself, a single, immense organism, moves toward a greater and higher harmony as more and more cells become conscious of their uniqueness. Life, then, is not Macbeth's "tale told by an idiot, full of sound and fury, signifying nothing." It is a grand orchestra in which discordant notes contribute to the total harmony.

V. S. Seturaman
is a professor of English literature in Madras, India

On one level, life is the process of seeking out and enjoying experiences—from the transcendent to the tragic. Life has a cyclical pattern of movement and appreciation; even when you're not doing anything, you're probably in a situation you sought.

On another level, life is the experience of the self's interaction with the world. The self can be broken down into three main elements and their corresponding activities: first, the heart (knowing compassion, receiving and giving love); second, the intellect (acquiring and digesting information); third, the senses (acting and being acted upon).

It is the soul, however, that focuses and inspires all three. The soul gives us resilience—an essential quality since we constantly have to rebound from hardship. It also enables human beings to develop because it is the medium through which we empathize. All the big pushes in humanity against destructive and exploitative forces have been caused by the soul reacting to these powers. Though people say things are getting worse, the kind of barbarism that was once accepted is not tolerated now. The soul has caused this development.

The meaning of life can't be understood without first looking at the self and its interaction with the world. In effect, this amounts to examining the inner workings of the soul of the universe.

Wynton Marsalis
is a jazz and classical trumpet virtuoso

During and after the U.S. invasion of Panama in 1989, we had to defend our neighborhood from looters and thugs who were roaming around shooting. We set up barricades. We used bricks and burned-out buses, whatever we could find. There were several exchanges of gunfire; I came close to getting hit. There was a great purpose during that period. This was my city and my country and my life I was defending. I had to try to restore some sense of order. I think we made a difference, in our own little way. That's the only thing you can hope for in life. There are things you can change. There are things you can't. And that's what it's all about: figuring out the difference.

Albert Joyce
is a lawyer in Panama City, Panama

Anonymous
LITHUANIAN PROTESTER
SELF-IMMOLATION, MOSCOW

After August 19, 1991, when our Russian parliament building was surrounded by tanks and the people prevailed, I realized that the meaning of life was hope. Our youth is our hope as we face this uncertain future. And we live so that we may immortalize ourselves in our sons and daughters. We live through their passions as well as their hardships. For me, this is the highest form of happiness and meaning.

Sergei Prikhodko
runs a vocational training school in Moscow

Kenneth Jarecke
HUNGER STRIKER AND SOLDIERS
IN STALEMATE, TIANANMEN SQUARE

(Overleaf)
Eugene Richards
CHILDBIRTH

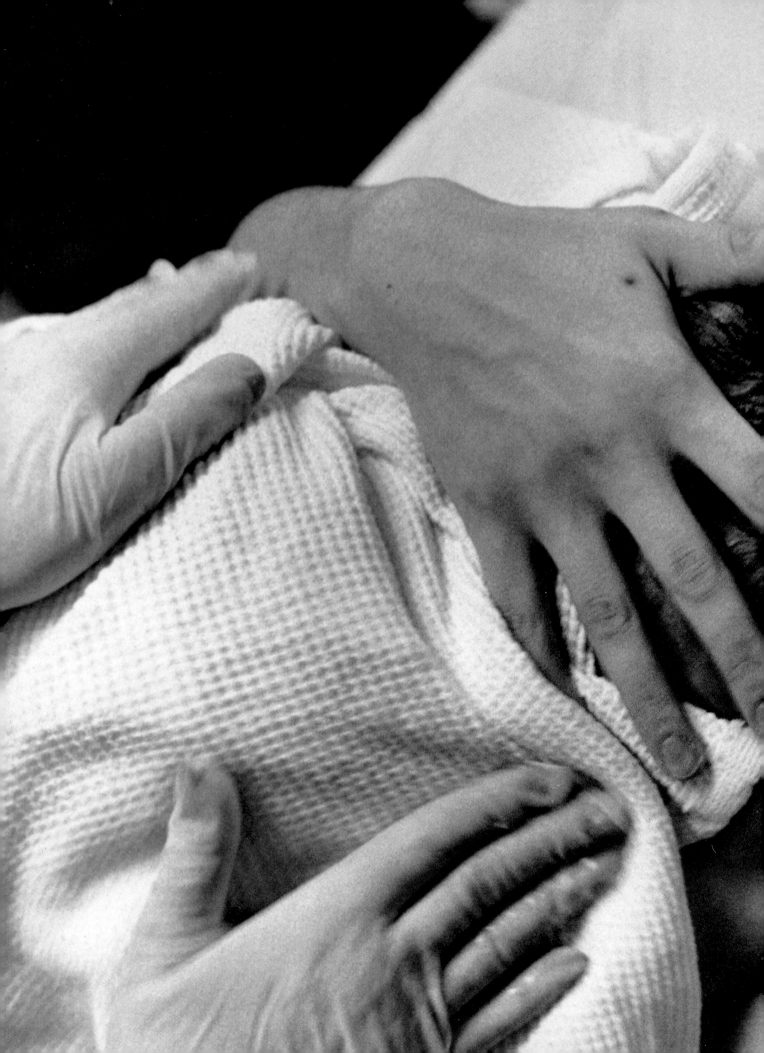

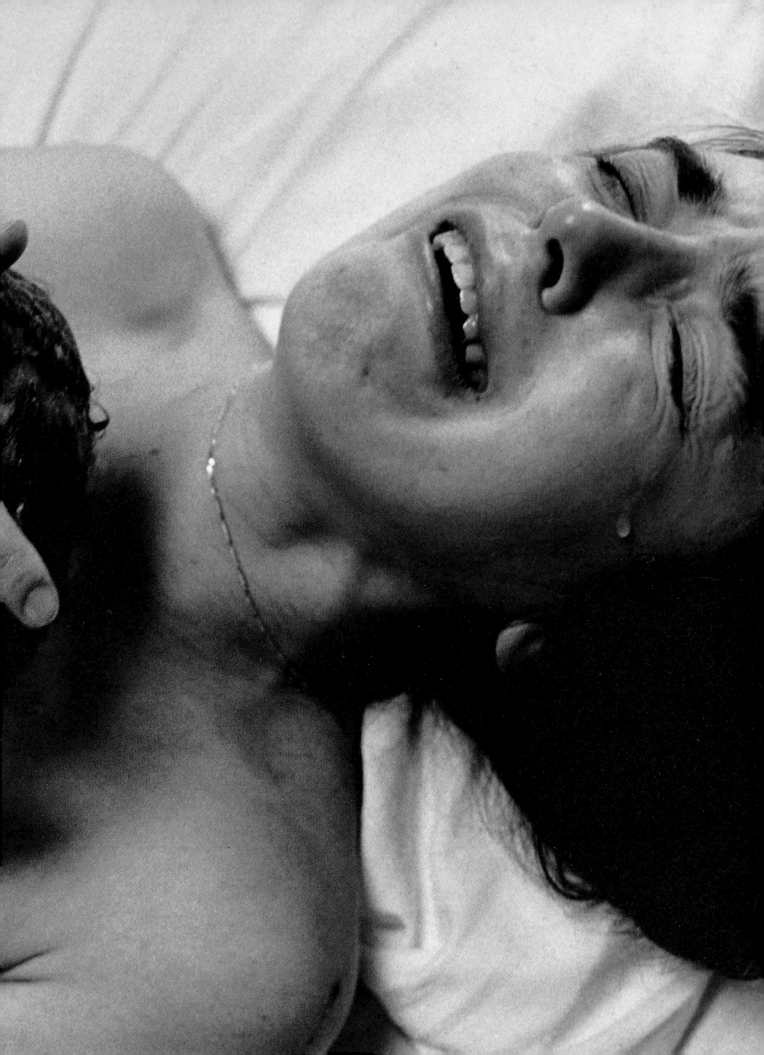

As a politician, my life has been a long pilgrimage to the highest goal of total service to humanity. My father's words keep echoing: "Your grandfather taught me politics of pride; your grandmother, politics of poverty. To you, my darling, I say, 'Believe only in the people. Work only for their emancipation and equality. My most rewarding achievements are those that have brought smiles of joy to the weary faces of our miserable masses, achievements that have brought a twinkle to the melancholic eye of a villager.' "

So that's the meaning of my life too. My commitment to the politics of the masses has required me to face incredible threats from the enemies of the people. My idea of living completely is spending every moment serving people and keeping alive in them the hope for a better tomorrow. I shall continue to seek freedom from want and fear, freedom of expression and worship. Tolerance, endurance and courage shall be unshakable parts of our political culture. What I seek for my country is what I would like to spread on a broader canvas across this planet.

Life is lived once and must be lived fully to justify one's creation.

Benazir Bhutto,
Pakistan's former Prime Minister, is the parliament opposition leader and head of the Pakistan People's Party

It is clear to me what my life has been about. It has been about risking my existence for the liberation of the state of Israel. It has been about struggling for a return to Zion and, moreover, helping freedom flourish in our newly reclaimed country (as Jews like to sing: "to be free in our land"). It has been about care and concern for the Jewish people, their security and that of Jews everywhere for generations to come.

And what, then, is life's meaning for all of us, collectively, Jew and gentile? Our raison d'être is entwined with morality, surely, a code of conduct and ethics laid down by God and, in turn, by man, in God's name. Each of us should realize and should exhibit through our actions the following truth: Moral influence and ethical responsibility are more important and more forceful and more lasting than mere power. We are here to be moral forces in the universe, in the world of nations, in our communities and in our families.

When it is all over, we will have understood that sometimes ideals mean more than life itself. I remember Meir Feinstein, who once said that having personally escaped Hitler's slaughter, he was not about to be cowed by a British regime in his own nation. "We were not spared," he said, "in order to live in slavery and oppression and to await some new Treblinka. We were spared in order to ensure life and freedom and honor for ourselves, for our people, for our children and our children's children. . . . There is a life that is worse than death and a death greater than life."

As I once wrote in my book *The Revolt*: "When Descartes said, 'I think, therefore I am,' he uttered a very profound thought. But there are times in the history of peoples when thought alone does not prove their existence. A people may 'think' and yet its sons, with their thoughts and in spite of them, may be turned into a herd of slaves—or into soap. There are times when everything in you cries out: Your very self-respect as a human being lies in your resistance to evil. *We fight, therefore we are!*"

Menachem Begin,
Zionist pioneer, was the prime minister of Israel

At the age of 16 I was deported to the Auschwitz concentration camp. I survived Auschwitz. Because Auschwitz had no meaning at all, and to even try to give it one would be to accept Auschwitz, I never again asked myself about the meaning of life.

Everything appeared to me as disorder and contradiction. How can one see the truth from the lie? How does one distinguish appearance from reality? I thus learned at Auschwitz that every human being can embody the good and the bad.

Who to believe? What to believe? As Europeans have realized over the past several years, no one can any longer ignore the fact that for decades, whole nations have deceived or have been deceived.

Nevertheless, without having searched for a meaning of life, I passionately love and want to believe in the progress of humanity. If man's imagination for destruction and killing is infinite, so too is his genius for belief in human progress. Because of the existence of Michelangelo, Mozart and Picasso, I can never lose hope in humankind. Because the beauty of a sunset can make me cry, our planet will always appear beautiful to me. Yet because the distress of a hungry child is as unbearable to me as was the anguish of Jewish children being led to the gas chambers, there remains in me a desire to fight misfortune and injustice. Perhaps it is this that gives meaning to my life.

Simone Veil
is a member of the European parliament and France's former Minister of Health

I was born and grew up in a state that not only claims it knows why I live but also takes upon itself the trouble of forcing me down the only true road toward my designated place in society, even dictating the course of my private life.

I believed that the meaning of my life and work came from following this idea. For a long time I was a novice in this ideological monastery, but with time I developed a deep distrust and my vision of the falsity of this system of "values" became clearer. At first I thought: "One can change things without changing one's faith." And I tried. Then I came to realize that the faith was faulty. Or, to put it exactly, I realized that the fault lay in the practical implementation of this ideal of seeking social justice; by appropriating monopoly to the socialist ideal, certain people had distorted it completely.

I have not betrayed my faith. Other people have. And, as a result, our roads have parted. Now I find meaning in my life by helping people understand how these paths have diverged so they can choose the right road themselves.

There must be some supreme, universal design. Each of us comes to life and stays in the world for a predestined period. Some leave forever, sometimes without a trace; others stay a long time, both in life and in memory. We remain longest—we make a difference—when we manage to act not for ourselves but for others.

It is possible to create good and evil. The greatest and most important thing a person can do is to understand that where good exists, evil also resides; what's more, one must strive to stay on the side of righteousness, doing one's best to promote good in the world.

Only you can make this choice. You alone will be held responsible—by other people, by your progeny and by history. I grieve over the fact that I did not come to understand this universal truth earlier in life.

Eduard Shevardnadze,

former Soviet Foreign Minister under Mikhail Gorbachev, founded the opposition Democratic Reform Movement

We are here to push the boundaries of ignorance, poverty, hunger and misery further back. Eventually, we hope these boundaries will disappear as we reach the state some call nirvana. (To my mind, nirvana is a stage at the end of many different lifetimes. It is a stage of happiness, contentment and gentleness that goes on, ad infinitum.)

How do we do this? By doing our individual best to support actions and programs that improve the lot of mankind. I think that once we have fulfilled our own material needs or have adequate means, we have an obligation to improve the conditions of life around us. Our own prestige should be of no concern, as we do what we believe is right and follow what we believe is the correct course.

Then, too, I think we all have a rare incident in our lives when there is a flash of light and a sense of God's work. I know in my life I felt it at the little chapel of Saint Francis of Assisi.

Claiborne Pell,

Democratic senator from Rhode Island, is chairman of the Committee on Foreign Relations

PK: Through the life and suffering and death of my sister Grace Patricia, who died of cancer at the age of ten and a half, I began to think a great deal about the meaning of life. I have asked, and I still ask, many questions. Why must children die as a result of the destructive and life-threatening policies of adults? Why must the human species face the prospect of extinction in this age of military and environmental catastrophe?

Since human beings have a moral conscience, a spiritual self and a physical self, we can choose among various options. And we are responsible for the consequences of our choices. We can put the common interests of humankind *above* the conflicts of ideological, racial, religious and national groups. We can bring together thought and feeling, politics and moral values, women and men, the underprivileged and the privileged.

GB: It is clearer what the meaning of life should *not* be. We are *not* here to hunt down happiness and success, oriented only toward ourselves, risking the lives and values of others and damaging the natural environment. Life is not selfish. Life strives to maintain harmony between humanity and nature. Life strives to heal.

PK: We must heal ourselves and the earth. We must take to heart the message of His Holiness the Dalai Lama, who says that the essence of life is the search for happiness. To realize this end, we must become one with the human family, one with the universe.

GB: For too many, a world void of violence, oppression, exploitation and war seems a mythical place. The meaning of life should be to make this illusion a reality. Only then will we fulfill the task Creation has given us. Only then will we use our short life for something more valuable than just growing old.

PK: We should live as if we were to die today. We should die as if we live forever.

Petra Kelly,

member of the German National Parliament, helped found the environmentalist Green Party, and

Gert Bastian,

former parliament and Green Party member, is a retired general and antinuclear activist

Marina Yurchenko
65TH WEDDING ANNIVERSARY

I've never read a book about this but I really understand about life . . . it comes from my brain like water when I speak . . . every day I must talk with people who have problems and they feel better . . . my cousin, after her brother died and her family couldn't pay for school, she wanted to jump into the well . . . I tell her to be strong, continue to study, if you are angry you will be sad and poison your body with the anger . . . life is too long—if you kill now, it will be stopped—be patient now, you will be happy . . . that's life—sometimes down, sometimes in high position—it's always like this . . . I'll teach you there's someone out there who needs you, you must live your life so that person can find you. . . .

Cokorda Tstri Ratih Tryani
is a Balinese dancer from Denpasar

Dirck Halstead
COUNTRY WEDDING, VERMONT

I observe all living things, from the spiders who spin their intricate webs to the bees who make geometrically perfect honeycombs, from the birds who know just when and where to migrate to the fish who find their spawning grounds, from the bats who navigate with exquisite radar to the dolphins who examine their environment with sonar. I know that intellect can never equal instinct in meeting a being's needs for survival.

Then why do I have intellect? If my function is merely to survive and preserve the species, would not instinct have been far superior? All intellect has really achieved for me is a measure of suffering known to no other living thing.

If I see a child with sleeves protruding far beyond his hands, trouser legs dragging behind him and a hat that reaches down to his chin, I know that he is wearing his father's clothes. When I observe the marvelous human intellect, I know it was designed for something much greater than mere survival. The meaning of all other animal life is survival. Hence, animals were designed to operate by instinct. The meaning of human life must be something beyond survival—even beyond comfort and pleasure, for these are better attained by instinct than by intellect.

Thus, the meaning of my life must be more than both survival and comfort. The meaning of my life is to use my unique intellect to search—yes, to search—for the meaning of my life.

Abraham Twerski,

a rabbi who operates a rehabilitation center for substance abusers in Aliquippa, Pennsylvania, is a direct descendant of the Baal Shem Tov, the 18th century founder of Hasidic Judaism

---

I once thought life's meaning was to surrender, to yield. I felt that to yield was to be swept along by, instructed by, made one with, even erased by "the unknowable." Perhaps I will believe this again.

Now I feel I can honestly know very little. Part of that small "knowable" is to recognize action and its consequences. I then must know how to act, how to use myself, how to exploit myself. To know this I must know the distinction between what I *can't* do and what I *won't* do. After that, the rest is simple: simply living.

Bill T. Jones,

choreographer and dancer, has performed in 22 countries

I have obligations both as a scientist (seeking advances in the material world) and as a religious creature (seeking truth in the realm of the spirit). As a scientist, I believe that the introduction of electricity has been of immense benefit, lessening much of mankind's grinding toil, enabling people to enjoy more fruitful lives. My life as an engineer has been dominated by the search for a really efficient method of generating and storing electricity. Coupled with new trends in solar energy, these processes will ultimately eliminate the need for burning fossil fuels. One of my main purposes as a man of science is to accomplish this goal before the scourges of air pollution become manifest.

In terms of religion, it is man's duty to continue his quest for the truth, especially with regard to the afterlife. Different religions seem to offer different opinions on this difficult subject. Just as scientists, in pursuit of truth, have made spectacular breakthroughs, surely we should use our brains in the spiritual field as well, not remaining content to accept the dogma laid down by previous generations. When you get to my age, nearly 87, you begin to wonder: Is the ultimate purpose of life on Earth to evolve spirit out of matter?

Francis Bacon,

British mechanical engineer, is the creator of the fuel cell, an electricity-producing device used widely in space travel

---

LIFE
To define what is "life" we'd begun
Using figments that science had spun,
Till whatever did sire us
Invented a virus
Which zapped us right back to square one.

BIRTH
Most parturition on earth
Bodes life as a joke without mirth;
Fowl yolk or placenta,
Each afterbirth meant a
Foul yoke to be borne after birth.

DEATH
Demise which the faithful esteem
As a call from a Being Supreme
Is instead to a skeptic
Just plain narcoleptic
Deep sleep—with decay—and no dream.

REINCARNATION
Repeated rebirth is a hoax
Believed in by misguided folks;
Because everyone knows
That a frog never shows
Any change though it constantly croaks.

MORALITY
One's ethical code should dispense
With dogma that's fixed and intense;
Without going to church you
Can manifest virtue
Through reason and plain common sense.

EPILOGUE
Hidden away in a gene
Or the brain, or some gland endocrine
Is LIFE's essence obscure—
But of one thing I'm sure:
It's a helluva good magazine!

Jack Kevorkian,

physician and creator of the "suicide machine," performed the first publicly disclosed doctor-assisted suicide in America

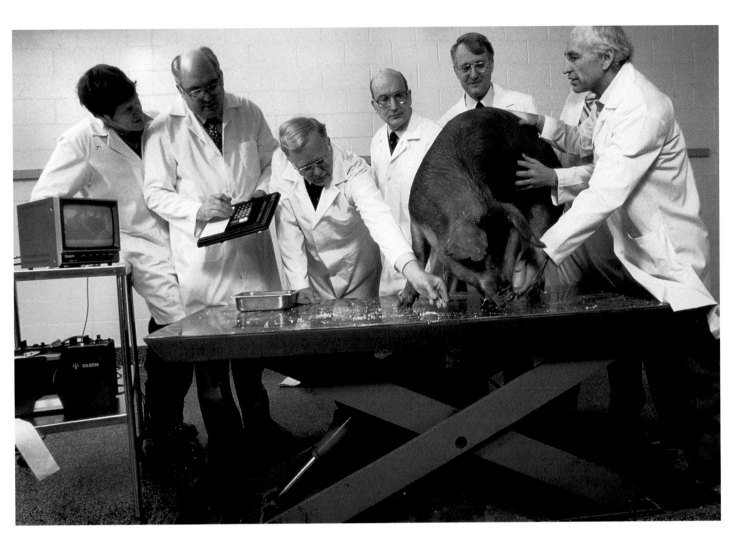

Co Rentmeester
SWINE SPECIALISTS AND SPECIMEN
AT THE UNIVERSITY OF ILLINOIS

One thing I always say about how people should live: "When you cast your bread upon the waters, you get back sandwiches." That's the best way to live. Whatever you put into life comes back.

When my husband went to the nursing home—he's 87—it was very hard for us. I was there today, and he said, "You know, I don't know what I would do if you didn't come here every day." I said, "I feel the same way. I couldn't live without seeing you."

Valeria Nunns
has retired from farming and
lives in Wahpeton, North Dakota

René Burri
TEHERAN TEAHOUSE

Vladimir Sichov
WASHERWOMAN IN VOLAGDA, U.S.S.R.

(Overleaf)
Harry Benson
BROOKLYN YESHIVA CLASS DANCES
THE HORA AT ISRAELI REUNION,
EFRAT SETTLEMENT

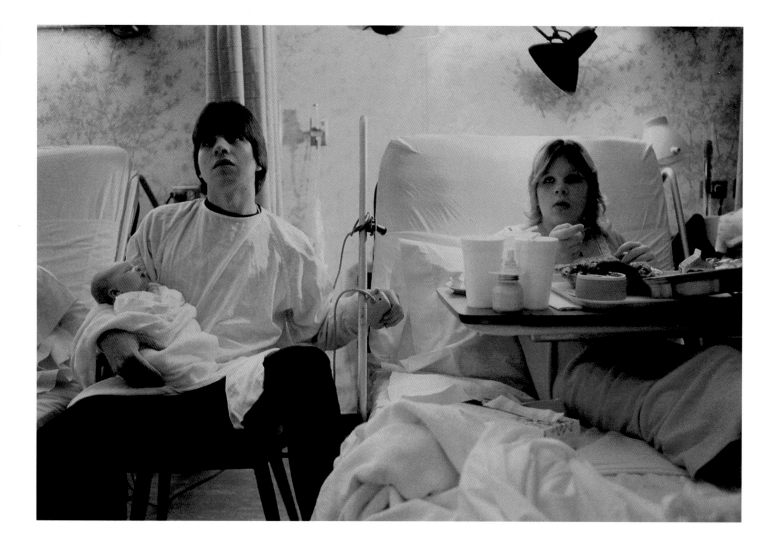

Michael O'Brien
TEENAGE PARENTS WITH NEWBORN

Peter Magubane
RIVER BAPTISM, SOWETO

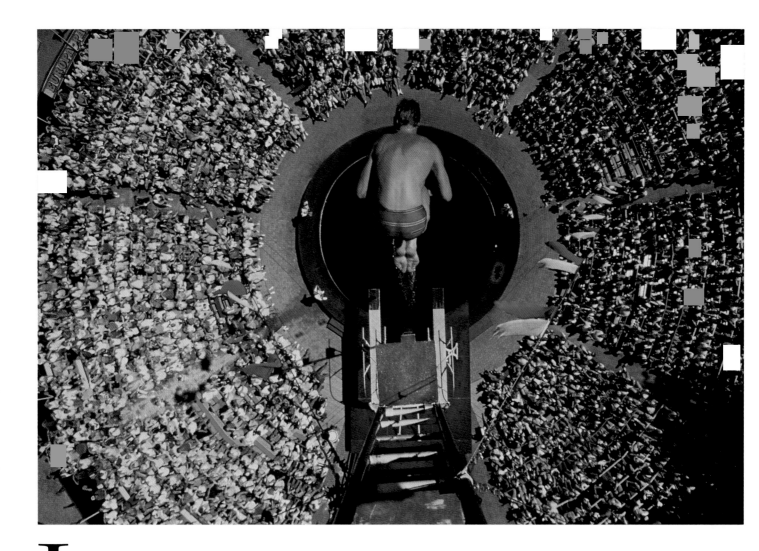

I t's not the distance that overwhelms people who race Hawaii's Ironman Triathlon. It's the relentless wind that blows across the lava fields. You're on one of the highest ridges, you see miles of repetitive road to Hawi, and you realize it's extremely hot and you're going straight into a 30-mile-an-hour crosswind. I've found that those who dwell on these conditions tend to fold. I always train for adversity. I consider adversity an asset, something to turn around to my advantage.

One of life's most important lessons is learning to put your losses in perspective and to savor your triumphs by riding on euphoria's wave. Have high goals and expectations; regard defeats as stages on the road to success by remembering the little victories that have gotten you where you are.

Dave Scott
is a six-time Ironman Triathlon winner

Michael Thoma
HIGH DIVER

Rich Clarkson
MIKE CONLEY, NCAA LONG JUMP
CHAMPIONSHIP FINALS, EUGENE, OREGON

Our presence, in relation to the universe at large, is as insignificant in its way as the dust on our shoes seems to us. Human existence is of no account whatsoever. It is purely accidental. It can neither be justified by any higher principle nor legitimized by any imaginative theology. We need not exist; the universe would hardly miss us. That alone is the dreaded truth, one we suppress and deny, imagining there must be a fundamental, as yet undetected reason for our being here. One can believe in some hidden purpose, thereby perpetuating one of man's dangerous addictions, his acceptance of outrageous madness in order to avoid being labeled a docile ant. But, unfortunately, an ant is what man is, and nothing more.

Human existence is a rope dance above a deep abyss. Whoever presumes to attain a firm footing by relying on the balancing pole (our irrational will to believe) may be fatally mistaken.

Günter Kunert

is a German poet and essayist

Confucius once said in six Chinese characters: "Not know life, how know death?" Any explanation of life's meaning is fallacious. There's no such thing. Even the word "life" is very doubtful. A virus lives. Does it have a meaning? Maybe. To kill us, I suppose. The first time I looked down a microscope in zoology class there were minute animals eating each other. Every second something is being eaten by something else.

When I was a teenager, I asked the wisest bishop I knew, "What is the purpose of life?" As far as I could see, it was the fulfillment of the nitrogen cycle. He said, "There is no particular purpose, but you must make one for yourself." I think his is the wisest answer. Decide what your destiny is and follow it. When Arjuna realized he'd have to fight people he loved and admired, Krishna advised: You are a warrior. Follow your destiny.

Earl Lu,

surgeon and painter, lives in Singapore

If I wanted to answer "What is the meaning of life?" I would have to anchor myself to some tradition. If I presented myself as a Zen Buddhist, I might answer by asking, "What is the meaning of *your* life?" To answer as a philosopher, I might lecture about certain value systems, etc. None of this would be an answer because the purpose of life is life itself. You cannot say there is life and then there is the purpose of life. To do so would be to split Man, to ignore fundamental unity.

I don't think that man has a particular aim. Rather, he should consciously, carefully coexist with everything alive. My own purpose is just to live, just to live. I wouldn't like to address the question of the meaning of life because in each situation there are many small aims, plenty of them entangled with one another, and all of them in some way make up life.

Rok Boleslav,

publisher of alternative books in Warsaw, coauthored Poland's first guide to natural childbirth

---

A group of us used to spend a lot of time getting drunk in the basement, discussing the meaning of life—a question that has caused more migraines than any other. We'd consider the creation theory. And the one about the thunderbolt that hits an arid pile of goop and somebody walks out with a tail and eventually we evolve. There's a belief some hold in the East that you have to go through seven levels to obtain perfection. And there's the idea of nirvana: a state where nobody dies, nobody gets sick, and you don't run into things with your car. You just float, and everything goes perfectly.

I remember hearing once about a professor who gave his class an exam consisting of one question: "Why?" Most of the students sat there, and they puzzled and they puzzled. But one guy was up and out in two minutes. His answer was: "Why not?"

"Why not?" seems to be a convenient stopping place. It suffices. It doesn't answer the question, but it gives a mere mortal a place he can pause and kind of put it in a box and say, "That's the best I can do." We're here because we are.

Glenn Lockhart

is a postal clerk in Fort Frances, Ontario, Canada

Allen Ginsberg
SPRING WINDOW

I sat for breakfast tea mornings a decade looking out my kitchen
table window, one day realized this was my World, familiar backyard
giant wet brick-walled undersea Atlantis garden waving with "Trees of
Heaven" (ailanthus, or "stinkweed), chimney pots along Avenue A, Stuyvesant
Town apartment top floors two blocks distant, I focus'd on clothes-
line raindrops: "Things are symbols of themselves," sd. Lama Chög-
yam Trungpa. August 18, 1984.
                                            Allen Ginsberg

This is the question that has caused man more anguish than any other since he became aware of his existence. It's the question of questions, the one that makes computers blow up.

The answer? In some cases, it is faith that's the key. In others, it is ideology. In still others, it is science. I formed my ideas in a climate that you could define as historic materialism. I don't have the gift of having faith, except, perhaps, a faith in life itself and in human beings, even with their bad and good, and in human history, which, even if it is cruel, bloody and horrendous, is also extraordinary. Certainly, man is a sort of miracle, born in a miraculous moment in a miraculous point of the universe because of a miraculous combination of matter and energy, perhaps casual? Perhaps not. It was, in fact, a marvelous chemical-physical process that gave birth to consciousness. The point of what happened on this planet wasn't the fact that one day a monkey stood up and began to walk upright, but the fact that he was *aware* of being, of getting up, of walking. He saw himself living and he had, you might say, a meaning—a miraculous moment of harmony that I can't imagine happened only on this planet. This moment gave us Bach. It gave us the ability to see that a star-filled sky might correspond to the infinite.

I do have some doubt. Perhaps all this miraculous impasto, this hodgepodge of energy and matter, might have something more to it. But I believe it is not for us to know. And so I am drawn to a concept of harmony that has something even more miraculous than the concept of God.

Lina Wertmuller,
internationally renowned Italian filmmaker, wrote and directed the provocative *Swept Away* and *Seven Beauties*

One of my earliest recollections is that of driving with my father, as the sun was coming up, across the Golden Gate Bridge. We were going to Marinship yard, where my father worked as a pipe fitter, to watch the launching of a ship. It was my birthday in the fall of 1943. I was four. When we arrived, the black, blue and orange steel-plated tanker was in way, balanced up on a perch. It was disproportionately horizontal and to a four-year-old was as large as a skyscraper on its side. I remember walking the arc of the hull with my father, looking at the huge brass propeller, peering through the stays. Then, in a sudden flurry of activity, the shoring props, beams, planks, poles, bars, keel blocks, all the dunnage, was removed, the cables released, shackles dismantled, the come-alongs unlocked. There was a total incongruity between the displacement of this enormous tonnage and the quickness and agility with which the task was carried out. As the scaffolding was torn apart, the ship moved down the chute toward the sea; there were the accompanying sounds of celebration, screams, foghorns, shouts, whistles. Freed from its stays, the logs rolling, the ship slid off its cradle with an ever increasing motion. It was a moment of tremendous anxiety as the oiler en route rattled, swayed, tipped and bounced into the sea, half submerged, to then raise and lift itself, but the witnessing crowd collected itself as the ship went through a transformation from an enormous, obdurate weight to a buoyant structure, free, afloat and adrift. My awe and wonder of that moment remained. All the raw material that I needed is contained in the reserve of this memory, which has become a recurring dream.

Richard Serra,
minimalist sculptor, is known for his site-specific public sculptures

The meaning of life is discovered through creativity and the knowledge that we are interconnected with the entire natural world. When we deny this, meaning is shattered. Our powers to destroy have been proved and we can no longer live out of harmony with nature, for we are at the Edge. It is time to engender love, beauty and poetic vision, all of which are expressions of the celebration of life. From this, meaning arises and our world can be transformed.

Marija Gimbutas,
Lithuanian-born archaeologist, developed the Goddess theory, which proposes that prehistoric European cultures were matrilineal and worshiped female deities

TO WHOM CAN I OPEN MY HEART?

I step outside to get a clear view
of this night's first stars, but something
  urgent
and full of an ancient, inexplicable pain
is aloft in the darkness of the hemlocks.
Again and again it makes its shrill cry of
  panic
One bird after dark.
What has befallen its nest, its wing, its sun?
So little to tell. Not even the word
  "tomorrow"
is world enough to offer myself
hearing it.

Tess Gallagher
is considered one of America's premier poets

Not taking myself too seriously seems to be the secret. It means getting out of myself and looking around, listening, becoming aware of what's going on. Feeling more than thinking. I'm going to sound like Snoopy when I say the big idea is that *we love one another,* but there it is.

Elmore Leonard
has been called America's
premier writer of crime fiction

April Saul
BOY WITH HIS MOTHER
AND NEW STEPFATHER

T

he meaning of life is felt through relationship . . .

Relationship with others and with one's own self.
From what it is at birth to whom we become as child,
Adult, parent, grandparent and, ultimately, as ancestor.
The meaning of life flowers through relationship . . .
Parenting teaching serving creating.
Learning from nature, the sages, our peers,
From our emerging selves in a state of becoming.

Jonas Salk,
developer of the polio vaccine, is currently researching an AIDS inoculation

Bob Sacha
SUMMER CAMP

(Overleaf)
Petr Rošický
MEETING AN EVANGELIST, PRAGUE

When my mother was 90 years old, she said, "I would still like to live a bit longer, just to see what happens next." Intellectual curiosity was, for her, a sufficient reason for living. She could also look back upon a life well spent in launching a variety of ventures that would continue to flourish long after she was gone. She helped write the legislation for the British Parliament that in 1919 opened the learned professions to women. She ran a birth control clinic in the 1930s, when this was an unusual avocation for a genteel English lady. She raised and educated a couple of children who still cherish her memory. She liked to say that we gave meaning to her life as much as she gave meaning to ours.

This is the central miracle of human life.

We are, in a small way, creators. We create language, we create music, we create scientific ideas, we create children. Our creations move out into the big world and become the heritage of future generations.

Once, when my daughter was nine years old and I came by her bed to say good night, she said, "Imagine that you meet a man who will answer three questions for you, and you know absolutely for certain that the answers will be right. What three questions will you ask?" In the child's voice I could hear my mother speaking.

Freeman Dyson,
British physicist and futurist, teaches at Princeton's Institute for Advanced Study

Marc Riboud
CAPPADOCIA, TURKEY

M y mother, a religiously
devout person, taught my brother and me
that life is a gift and with it comes
responsibilities to others as well as to
oneself. My father, a scientist, would often
say that life is also a mystery, one to be
explored constantly.

Their sense of things still lives in me as
I try to be as decent a husband and
father as possible, regretting mistakes and
hoping to learn from them. A good deal
of the meaning in my life rests in my
children—in their hopes and ideals, in the
concreteness of their fine lives. In my
working life, as a doctor and teacher, I also
try to live up to the values my parents
handed on, values I hope to hand on
to others: the struggle to embody loving-
kindness in a life, for all the prideful vanity,
the "unreflecting egoism" as George Eliot
put it, with which we all must contend.

Life's meaning amounts to how
we actually manage to live it with others.

Mark Sennet
EDMUND PAUL HALLEY SR.
AND GREAT-GRANDSON RYAN AWAIT
THE RETURN OF HALLEY'S COMET

Robert Coles,
Harvard psychiatrist and Pulitzer Prize–winning
author, wrote *Children of Crisis*

When my husband, Benigno, was imprisoned at the start of martial law in 1972, we thought life was over. We could not understand this injustice. But I asked myself what sins Jesus had committed to make His sacrifice justified, and I realized we are all faced with injustices. If we have faith, we can overcome every difficulty. My husband had not been a religious person, but once he was in jail, God was the only one he could turn to. Through reading the Bible and putting his destiny in God's hands, he became strongest at the time he felt weakest.

God created us in His image with the purpose of showing that we all belong to Him, that He is almighty and that we should try our best to be like Jesus Christ. Through faith, I have come to think of my suffering and my family's as part of our life with Christ, rather than punishment from God.

At the end of a long day of addressing so many seemingly unsolvable problems, you think to yourself, "What is it all about?" And yet, when I can get a group of farmers low-interest loans and the right technology to improve their lives, I feel tremendously fulfilled. The high point in life, I guess, is being able to do something for your fellow man.

Corazon Aquino
is the President of the Philippines

I have had many experiences that were very painful and joyful at the same time. I lived the extreme when I was put in prison because of my controversial writing and criticism of the governing system. I was put in jail without trial; I did not know whether to expect execution or life imprisonment. When you face the danger of death, you know life. You cannot know white except beside black. When I faced death, I knew life, I loved life. I didn't want to lose one precious minute, even in jail. Through my imagination, my brain cells, I transcended the jail. Life is this ability to go on in spite of death, to be free despite imprisonment.

I once worked in a mental hospital. When you face madness, you know rational thinking. I learned that mad people are sometimes much more intelligent than sane people. The sane, who are often oppressed, inhibited and false, are afraid to ask new questions about life. But mad people are brave. They want to live life to its fullest, but they are not allowed. When you see people living at the depths of existence, you understand life.

To me, the meaning of life is to live with passion, to live honestly, to believe in yourself, to be spontaneous. I don't believe in the afterlife as religions describe it. I believe in living my present life fully.

Life is very ancient. It is related to the evolution of our bodies. This is especially true for women since women can reproduce life itself. Life for me, as a human being, as a woman, as a writer and as a psychiatrist, is to allow my body, mind and spirit to thrive. As human beings we are split by society, patriarchy, class, religion, authority, power, men, money and technology. We have been split into mind, body, spirit and the so-called soul. To live means to bring all these fragments back together, to be one, to be myself, Nawal el Saadawi.

Nawal el Saadawi,
psychiatrist, author and leading
Egyptian feminist, is head of the Arab
Women Solidarity Association

As a young Jew in the Soviet Union, my hobby was chess, my profession was cybernetics and my religion was science. I believed that bringing more logic to the world would save us from totalitarianism, Communism and all the other "isms" depriving us of freedom. Closed in the ivory tower of science, I was trying to save myself from bloody ideological storms, and there I did find satisfaction for my intellectual curiosity, but not peace for my soul.

Then I decided to be myself, starting from the most simple and natural thing: expressing out loud what I thought and felt. The rest came by itself. You start from the simple and you find everything else: your past and your future, the history to which you belong and the country where you want to live. The Soviet system reacted with unyielding logic. One after another, the walls were raised around me—the camp, the prison, the cell, the punishment cell. And with every wall, there was less information, less light, less air, less food. The choice offered to me was surprisingly clear and coldly logical: Take back your words, and you are free.

In the darkness and quiet of the punishment cell there was finally peace. You discover that you are connected not only with your family and your people but with all those that have lived before you and those that will live after you. You realize that everything you say, and everything you do, influences the fate of all people. You can say no to the logics of chess, and answer to another set of logics— the belief that all human beings are created in the image of God and that the actions of each one affect the present, and future, of all. And this desire, to live up to a great design, makes you truly free.

Natan Sharansky,
Soviet dissident now living in Israel,
is a spokesman for Soviet Jewry

Neil Leifer
PRISONER, ATTICA, NEW YORK

W

e are here because in this part of the universe time is trained to stop. It could be that we are in touch with a sort of tame, domesticated time. Life cannot survive in time that flows, or while it flows. Life survives only when time stands still. We can imagine eternity descending from God like a blessing, resembling a kind of light that never becomes old, as some Byzantine monks believe. We can imagine time coming from Satan, standing to the left side of the temple.

So it could happen someplace, somehow, that eternity and time would meet at a golden intersection. At the very heart of the cross, where eternity and time would connect, time would stop to be blessed by eternity. And that, in fact, is our present. Consequently, the present is the very portion of time that has stopped. Life survives only in the present. The past, therefore, consists of moments during which time has previously stopped; the future, of moments during which time will subsequently stop.

So here we are. We are here because in this part of the universe time stops and makes life possible. Perhaps we can imagine a time that is not lined up to intersect eternity, a time that would seem sterile to our way of thinking. In such a region of the universe, we would not be in a position to exist since our dominant features are those of life and death.

Of course, some of my protagonists have different opinions.

Milorad Pavić,
Serbian novelist, short-story writer and poet,
is the author of *Dictionary of the Khazars*

Roger Malloch
SWING

Calderón said: "All life is a dream, and dreams themselves are only dreams." Ever since man has existed, he has sought life's meaning. Who are we? Why do we live? What is our goal? Has man been made in the image of God or God in the image of man? Each concept has its opposite: life / death, yes / no, light / shadow.

Life's meaning rests in the eye of the beholder and in our constant desire to approach perfection. Life is so immense and complex that there is no one truth, only the rule of destiny. Regardless, here are attempts at answers.

We do not choose life; life chooses us. Yet we try to follow our destiny, our passion, our drive. We must live every minute as if it is our first and our last. Never give to receive in return. Never be calculating. Give more than you receive.

Let your judgment, above all, be guided by compassion. The meaning of life lies in our desire to help others. Let us show compassion for those weakened by compromise while honoring those who are exceptionally enlightened and humane.

Earthly life is an eternal miracle. In a moment of grace, we can grasp eternity in the palm of our hand. This is the gift given to creative individuals who can identify with the mysteries of life through art. It is a divine gift, this spirit of humanity. It is the fight for light over shadow.

Marcel Marceau
is France's maestro of mime

Anthony Suau
ASLEEP ALONG THE ROADSIDE, MOLDAVIA

W e are each put on this earth to make a particular contribution to humanity. Some as teachers; others as housewives, executives, athletes, doctors, farmers, actors or politicians. The list is endless. Although God, the Almighty, has a plan for every one of us, He gives us choices. It is our responsibility to make the best of those choices in order to achieve our ultimate purpose.

God gave me a talent to do gymnastics. But I had to choose to completely dedicate a number of years of my life to the sport in order to make the most of that talent.

As simple as it sounds, we all must try to be the best person we can: by making the best choices, by making the most of the talents we've been given, by treating others as we would like to be treated. If we live by God's rules, during our relatively short time on this earth, we will be rewarded greatly with eternal life with God in heaven!

Mary Lou Retton
was the first American woman to win an Olympic gold medal in gymnastics

A fter thinking about this question for some time, I've decided that the simplest answer is the best: Life really doesn't have much meaning without death. Death gives each moment its value. It makes each instant precious and meaningful. When you understand how valuable each moment is, you begin to act accordingly.

Why are we here? To reproduce, that seems clear.

Elle Macpherson
is an Australian-born model and cover girl

I can remember when the notion first occurred to me that my own life had any meaning at all. I was at my high school graduation, and I suddenly realized that it was up to me, and no one else, to make something of myself—that I could turn my juvenile fondness for puttering with living things into a profession, becoming a kind of person that, naively, I defined as a biologist. Gradually I learned that there is a lot more to personhood than one's profession and, in time, I acquired a more complex, richer self-image. That salutary development was itself the outcome of simply being a biologist: someone with work to do, tasks to be performed not only for my own purposes, but for society's as well. My own personal growth was generated not only by my relations with others, but also by what I did as a member of society—in the classroom, the laboratory and the arena of public discourse.

This has taught me a wonderful lesson. My duty to myself and to those close to me coincides with my duty to society. My own life and fate are embraced by human history, which, despite its agonizing trials and catastrophic failures, is nevertheless a source of optimism.

Barry Commoner,
author, political activist and former candidate for the U.S. presidency, is one of America's leading environmentalists

T he "less moral" way can be very tempting. Like everyone, I am always in a kind of battle between my lower self (the part of me tied to society's pettiest goals: greed, selfishness, narrow-mindedness) and my higher self (the part of me that cares for others and acts for the benefit of the community). The Koran guides me. It teaches that some of the reason we're here is to exercise personal responsibility, to evolve the higher self and to influence that development in others.

Kareem Abdul-Jabbar,
basketball great, led the Los Angeles Lakers to five NBA championships

W hy are we here?'' may be the wrong question to ask because, as an organ with finite capabilities, the mind cannot consider the infinite possibilities the question implies. It would be like asking my four-and-a-half-year-old daughter to explain Einstein's theory of relativity. It requires a tremendous leap of faith to come up with a reason for being. And I don't think anybody can have an answer he believes in with rock-solid confidence.

In trying to concoct a reason for existence, we've created theologies. Given my travels as a tennis player, I have been exposed to Buddhism, Shintoism, Confucianism, Taoism, Islam, Christianity, Judaism, Santería, animism. And I have always been perplexed to find that most of the world's great organized religions tell you they have the only answer. Christ said, "No one cometh unto the Father but by me." In Islam, Allah is God and Muhammad is His one true prophet. I kept thinking, "Hey, somebody's got to be wrong!"

Despite my skepticism that any one religion can provide universal truths, I have synthesized many faiths and come up with some basic ideas. One is that all we see around us, living or inanimate, could not have come from nothing. There had to be an original cause. The second idea is that my life is part of a continuum that goes back as far as life itself has been around and that will be around after I'm gone.

Arthur Ashe,
tennis player and sports consultant, was the first black man to win the Wimbledon and U.S. Open championships

It may have been the longest journey I have ever made. Confused, shocked and helpless, I mourned quietly, tears rolling down my face, as the Coast Bus raved down the Nairobi-Mombasa road, a road that, for years, had been a symbol of home and family unity to me. Nothing seemed to matter. My shattered mind kept returning to the conversation I had had with my brother earlier in the morning. He had asked me to return. All was not well. Mother was no more. I tried to reason with myself. Or was it with God? How could he have allowed it to happen—again? After all, my father had died six years earlier and my sister had died at 20, 12 years before. Now my mother! Was he so mean that after all our prayers for her to live, he had let her die of cancer?

In my mind's eye, during that fateful bus ride, I saw the warmth that our home and extended family had always offered. Cousins and brothers reunited at school holidays. Days spent on the farms or looking for firewood. Nights gathered around a fire in Grandmother's grass-thatched hut at the entrance to our village. Suddenly home was going to be cold, empty! Life would be meaningless without her presence. Just days before I had been thrilled by the thought of taking gifts to her. She deserved everything from me, from us. Couldn't she have lived, I wondered, to see the results of her sacrifices? In the evenings of my youth, girls would put water-filled containers on their heads and boys would place theirs on their shoulders as we walked home from the distant primary school. And Mother had watched with a glowing pleasure as our hardships turned into a blessing, as one of my brothers and I attended university.

Where was God's role in all this? Did he care? Was he happy to make my family suffer? It did not matter whether, as many African people believe, her death had been caused by some bad omen, witchcraft or predestined phenomena. What really mattered was the loss. I swore to myself that there could never be a God, that it no longer mattered if he existed. I called it quits, as the bus sped home.

My experiences have left me with a conviction that life is a bundle of contradictions. One moment you are at your height, appreciating your achievements, values and experiences; the next, you are diving into the sea, deprived of the very essence of life's meaning. Out of these fluctuating experiences, however, you somehow live on, perhaps stronger, perhaps not. I have since lost my brother, who perished en route to my wedding send-off party. It still surprises me that despite my anger and endless questioning of God's wisdom I still find consolation. I believe our existence, our losses and our achievements are lessons for ourselves and others, lessons that complement our purposes on earth. They emphasize our vulnerability but, in turn, help us realize we have no individual willpower over the force of fate.

Jemimah Mwakisha,
of the Taita tribe, grew up
in the Kenyan village of Kirutai

AIDS is the result of biological determinism. That is clear. It is not the result of a decision from Above. If we held such a belief, we would be reverting to medieval times, praying and lighting candles.

Am I optimistic about AIDS? It depends on the day. I still hope that someday we will find an explanation that will lead to a definitive therapeutic approach, eventually allowing us to cure people. At the same time, we have to remind ourselves that AIDS poses a major threat to existence in the coming century. Man evolved in a precise manner over millions of years. And in the modern age, as we accelerate changes in our environment, we speed up time, prompting enormous changes in human life. We must realize the peril: With AIDS as a starting point, humanity might be completely swept away. It would take time, of course. But behind the visible virus, there might be other elements that we don't know and have no means of fighting medically.

I've been very moved by AIDS patients. I remember one 13-year-old hemophiliac. For several years the boy remained in good condition but then succumbed to AIDS. He had become a skeleton, his eyes fixed in a blank stare. His parents had opened the windows in his room so he could see blue sky outside, but he was no longer a living being. He already seemed to have gone beyond. He died the next day.

Experiences like that leave you feeling you have an obligation to help others. And yet, as a scientist, I also feel humiliated. In the face of AIDS, the healing wizard is suddenly, unbearably impotent. Encounters with patients help me appreciate that human life spans but a wink in time. No sooner do you open your eye than you have to close it. You look around, take stock of the complexity and immensity of the universe, and then you leave. In the course of a normal life, you store an incredible quantity of information—music, art, science—that can disappear in a flash when you have a stroke or heart attack. Then you die. What a waste. Your son or your daughter has to relearn everything you learned, starting from scratch. It's ephemeral, enormously inefficient and very, very unfortunate.

What, then, do we live for? What, then, should we aim for? I would like to live to 150. Perhaps science will someday permit us to prolong life, changing human behavior and civilization in the process. I see this as desirable. I would like to have time to write—I have a message to pass on. After all, the best way to live on is through one's works. That's what we hope for, no? To survive your death through your contributions. To leave a trace.

Luc Montagnier,
head of the AIDS-Retrovirus department
at the Pasteur Institute in Paris,
codiscovered the virus that causes AIDS

David Malin
Zeta Orionis, the Horsehead
Nebula and NGC 2024

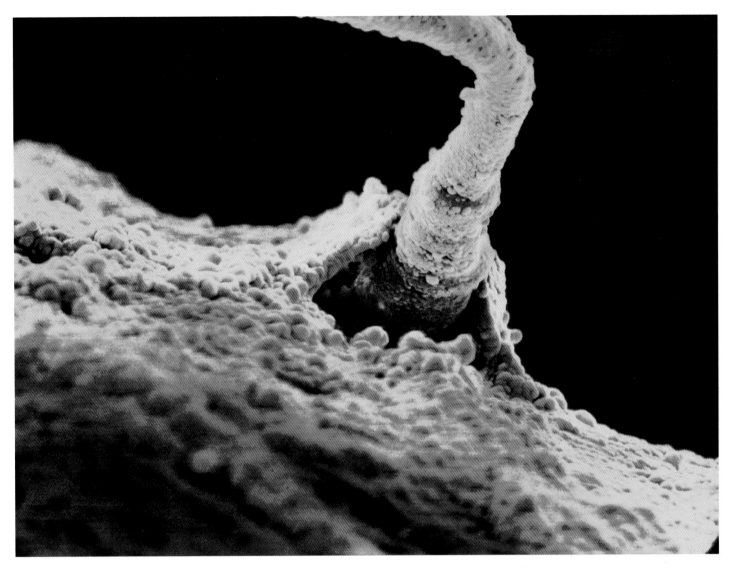

The meaning of life is ours to create, again and again, for every individual and generation. Only by creating and re-creating the fabric of meaning can we live. We are, of all the species on this planet, the one that lives by the creation of meaning, as bees must manufacture honey or spiders must make the stuff of their webs, spinning vast geometrical landscapes. Thus, there is no single text that can be consulted to find the meaning of life, nor does it exist as a hidden code waiting to be teased out like the sequencing of the human genome. Meaning is what human beings create from what they see and hear and remember, partly private and partly shared within our overlapping lives. Meaning is what we weave with each other and with patterns passed down from the past, selecting, discarding, embroidering, twisting the threads together to draw every man and woman and child into a larger whole.

Mary Catherine Bateson,

American linguist and anthropologist, is the author of *With a Daughter's Eye,* a memoir of parents Margaret Mead and Gregory Bateson

Lennart Nilsson
Sperm Penetrates Ovum

R

opes . . .

As a newborn, I toyed with the umbilical cord.

As a child, I teased grown-ups with knots of malice their incredulous fingers could never untangle. Splicing solitude with altitude, I rigged a destiny far above the College of Normalcy. No sooner had my claws clung to the tightrope than commanders were ordering me down: "We know better! Follow the rules!" They fastened nooses. They cast snares. Fortuitously, the enchanting roar of the unwinding spool of rapture altered my hearing.

"Conquistador of the Useless."

On the high wire my existence has meaning. All is composed, serene, faultless, profound. Below boils the cacophony of restraints. And who can tell what looms above?

I reside in an unfinished Gothic cathedral at the heart of a brutal metropolis, where I am never far from the tapping of mallets on chisels. The carving of limestone blocks on the Portal of Paradise, tock-tock, tock-tock, reminds me that it is still possible to behold miracles from the deck of our miserable, sinking planet. On I battle against myself, against myself, against most of you, pulling the cable a fraction of an inch to carry my boat over the mountains: bare-handed, barefoot, handcuffs clanking, shackles rattling.

Prisoner of an incurable disease: an excess of passion.

Chains . . .

Philippe Petit,
French aerialist, is artist-in-residence at Manhattan's Cathedral of St. John the Divine

I

n 1989 I spent 131 days in an underground cave in Carlsbad, New Mexico, communicating via computer with researchers 50 feet above me. I kept a diary during my stay, and I think the following passage expresses my thoughts about the meaning of life. The only possible answer one can give comes in the form of yet another question. This process repeats continuously until the cycle closes.

Actual date: February 17, 1989, 7:30 p.m.
Perceived date: February 4, 1989, 11 a.m.

They asked me if I believe in God.

I believe in the dignity of being and, even more so, of becoming. Unlike the horse, says Pirandello, man knows he must die; and this knowledge accompanies him every day. Man does not resign himself to disappearing, however. He tries, in any way possible, to leave a trace of his passage. He clings to the heavens and to reincarnation. He wants to emblazon history with his legacy. These very words, which tomorrow may be ashes, yearn to be savored lest they fall into obscurity.

Death may not be an end but only a passage, a dimensional leap. And what if, once free of the slavery of three and four dimensions, once released from space and time, we were to discover unimaginable realities beyond our poor five senses? What if we encountered not hells and heavens, but transformations of energy through which we continued to exist in totally inconceivable, illogical ways? What if we became images, sensations, ideas, wavelengths . . . ?

If I were an image, I would like to be a mirage.

If I were a sound, I would like to be a tormenting and disquieting solo played on Andean panpipes.

If I were an idea, I would like to be a doubt.

If I were light, I would like to be the deceptive reverberation of twilight.

If I were a flower, I would like to be a caper, splendid and poor, ephemeral and tenacious.

Stefania Follini,
Italian interior designer, holds the women's record for solitary cave dwelling

O

rphans and oxen know why; we're here to work or die.

I was seven when my parents died, and I cried so hard I was lost for days. Then hunger found me and guided my steps. Hunger became my guardian angel, my teacher. People say hunger is cruel, but I think hunger is honest.

When I was a little orphan I saw a sow devour her litter. I screamed and threw stones and hit it with a stick, but she kept eating the babies. The old lady who owned the pig ran over to protect it. She was proud of that sow. Its litters were large and fetched a good price. It made her a woman of property instead of simply poor.

The old lady saw the sow's face smeared in blood and didn't say a word. She raised up her ax and crashed it into the pig's head again and again until it was dead. Then she stared at the ax and the pig and the babies until she took my hand and started walking down the street. We were both all covered with blood, and she was still holding the ax.

At the market people made way for us as if we were generals or kings. She instructed the butcher on every detail, knuckles, ears, intestines, snout, tail and feet. Each part was to go to a different family. She ordered me to help the butcher because if I learned how to slaughter I'd always eat meat.

She was the most wise and just woman I ever knew but after that day people called her crazy. They said she lost her mind and couldn't be trusted. They forgot about the sausages and chops she gave them. Instead they remembered how she walked around town all covered in blood while swinging an ax in the air.

Rosa Gonzalez
sells Aymara Indian crafts and talismans on the streets of La Paz, Bolivia

Cristina García Rodero
LAS POTENCIAS DEL ALMA
(THE POWERS OF THE SOUL)

Mitsuaki Iwago
LIONESS ATTACKING ZEBRA,
THE SERENGETI

If you see a tree being destroyed, you can smell and feel the death, the sadness of it. Because it's alive, as birds are. And mosquitoes. And you and I. Energy is never created or destroyed. When one thing dies, life is that energy, the soul, that is transformed into another form.

Look at you. You're sitting, talking. I put a cat beside you. She sits and meows. I give her food, she extends her paw. Then you have your hand around her neck and snuff her out, and the energy goes into some other form. And I do the same to you, my hand around your neck, and you go. What is the difference? Animals kill, we do too. We call it the Iraqi war, Vietnam. All kinds of things, and then we all die.

Nature used to do a better job with plagues and the like. Now Western man wants to control fate, prolonging life through technological advances. But he's tampering with the balance of nature. If this goes on, eventually he'll have to leave it to nature's diseases to control population. Or he'll have to adopt cruel methods like encouraging people to eliminate themselves. If animals or insects get too numerous, we allow hunting or use pesticides. I think man will have to devise a "process of choice," eliminating all but the fittest.

Take my own mother. A working woman with a challenging mind, she confronted the church and our village taboos. She encouraged women to refuse the bonds men put on them. Now she's 86 and in a wheelchair. I'm happy to see her, but she's a burden to herself and her society. She's done her job. I'm not going to eliminate her; you'd call me a murderer. But the old lady Eskimo will wander into the cold if there isn't enough food for the young. I think the old should be encouraged to make their own choice or else the human race is going to go. If the race goes, who'll be left to be sad about it?

I remember seeing a play in which God and the Devil, administrator and technician, start the creation. Halfway through, God decides to take over and finish it all with his angels. The Devil says, "That's why you've got such a mess. Technically, it's incomplete. And *I* get all the blame." I believe everything's a mess and our job is to create a form of harmony, a mixture of beauty and love. The more man gives love, the more he grows, the more love he has to give. But there is a limit to your love. Most of the time what you do is forgive and tolerate and grow above the pettiness that an otherwise weak man would let grow inside him until it destroyed him. You must be a wolf, a free, venturing spirit.

Nabil Sawalha
is a popular Jordanian actor, educator and hotelier

The market mechanism has gone completely out of control. It regulates itself. All it wants to do is produce more and more and more. And one day this simply has to come to a stop. In the relatively near future, in order to deal with the population explosion, governments will have to resort to things we can hardly imagine right now. It's going to be a very unpleasant, messy and nasty world. I think we're headed for a lot of trouble around the year 2050.

In complex societies no one knows the overall picture. And governments often deceive us. No one can be in total control of the information content of his society, but unless he is, how on earth can he deal with these things? What happens is that no one deals with them.

The aborigines, on the other hand, live in small groups. They are all in a position to deal with what they face in their environment. I believe that people should live in small communities (no bigger than 3,000), work toward good social relations and not mess with the environment. Foreign trade should be banned. You should live by your own community's resources. If you haven't got too many—too bad. Instead of having one huge market system, we'd have little separate communities. Each would act as a baffle plate against the other.

Muhammad Ruslan bin Abdullah
is a retired assistant director of the Department of Aboriginal Affairs in Kuala Lumpur, Malaysia

I have believed for some time now that Nietzsche was correct in saying that human beings would rather have The Void for meaning than be completely void of meaning. If I could offer anyone wisdom on the subject of life's purpose, it would be this: Confront the absolute meaninglessness of existence and find the stoicism and self-control to go on in the face of it. This doesn't mean that one should be a nihilist or that one should believe in "nothingness itself." Nor should one derive any joy from living this way. Joy's not the point. I would never tell anyone to "rejoice in the abyss" or "enjoy the infinite sense of repetition." Rather, one should believe in striving, in enduring. We are here to endure, to the end. That is, perhaps, the most honest thing we can do. Nietzsche said: Just take one step beyond and forgive yourself everything. He was saying, in effect: Perform an act of grace toward yourself, and when you have done that, the entire drama of the fall and redemption will be acted out within yourself.

In Shakespeare's *King Lear,* Edgar says to his father, Gloucester: "Men must endure / Their going hence, even as their coming hither. / Ripeness is all." That statement does not express any religious stance whatsoever. Instead, it acknowledges that there is a kind of fundamental meaninglessness and that all one can do is keep on.

Harold Bloom,
Yale's Sterling Professor of Humanities, is America's best-known literary critic

Kaia Means
FATHER DISCOVERS HIS BABY,
EXTRACTED FROM SAN FRANCISCO
EARTHQUAKE WRECKAGE

David Parker
SWAT RESCUE, YUBA CITY, CALIFORNIA

What do we live for? I don't know. All I know is that we are a product of organic evolution, an incredibly mysterious process, unique to this particular planet, the only planet alive in our solar system. Just to take part in this process, to contemplate it, is a marvelous experience, a profoundly religious one.

I do not believe in a transcendental creator. I believe in Creation. To me, nature itself is sacred, and science is the contemplation of the divine beauty of the universe. As a scientist, I know that the universe behaves according to well-defined laws that are universal and eternal, that is, unchangeable, laws that cannot be transgressed. In order to discover these laws, science must carry on a clean, honest dialogue with the universe. There is no cheating in science as there often is in technology and many forms of religion.

When life first structured itself in the primeval oceans, it was just a soup of organic molecules. A billion years later, organisms of the complexity of modern bacteria came about. Next came the diversification of life forms, leading to the millions of species we have today. Every species, then, is the result of millions of years of accumulated natural wisdom. Every species goes back to the beginning of life and, in a broader sense, to the beginning of the universe. True naturalists, when they look out of the window of a plane and see land or desert or ocean or woods, feel responsible. Some even consider the planet a living being, a being that they call by a name: Gaia. They see the evolving world as something sacred.

My personal destiny is unimportant. What does it matter if I die tomorrow? What matters is to realize that one's existence is a fantastic privilege to participate in this inexplicable process of evolution, a process that, if we don't destroy or seriously maim it, has another five billion years to go.

José Antonio Lutzenberger

is Brazil's Secretary of Environment

Michael Friedel
XINGU INDIANS SPEARFISHING ON THE AMAZON

The world's attitude is that leprosy is something ugly. After I got leprosy, at nine, I had red knobs all over me. I had a lot of pain. My hands started to curl. My friends stopped coming around. I was very sad. I just wanted to die because of the rejection and the pain. Now I've had treatment, seven operations. I feel normal. I have a family: a lovable husband and a child. I go to church and mix with people outside, and they accept me. I feel my life has fullness.

Yes, God is fair. I'm actually glad I got leprosy. If I hadn't, I wouldn't have come to know God.

I realize everybody has problems, but we don't have to always have them in front of us. We can put them under our feet and stand on them, gaining strength in having struggled with them. I realize we must look at people the way God looks at them—as lovable.

Rabiap Boonma
decorates Christmas cards in Chiang Mai, Thailand

My illness demanded its due. A leg amputation would offer the best chance for survival. Suddenly I could take nothing for granted. "Why?" I asked. "How will my life now proceed?" I posed similar questions when a dear friend died and, for the first time, I was confronted with the incomprehensibility and finality of death. At such moments, you can only depend on yourself; everything around you continues as before. The world is not impressed.

In every emergency situation, the vulnerability of your own little life becomes palpably apparent. The risk of withdrawing at these moments is considerable, a danger that increases as our world grows more complex and obscure. Satirist Kurt Tucholsky made the point that the condition of all human morality can be summed up in two sentences: "We ought to. But we don't."

We ought to and we *should*. We must talk rather than maintain our comfortable silence. We must walk through life with tolerant, open minds, instead of wearing blinders. Every man and every woman must assume responsibility for his or her role in protecting our environment and in enabling us to live together peacefully. Ultimately, this is where our efforts count: where humble things are indistinguishable from big things, where individual spheres meet overriding spheres.

Karen Gesierich,
German swimmer who lost her leg to bone cancer, has won medals in international competitions for the disabled

I have never been seriously in doubt as to why I am here—or, anyhow, why I believe I should be here. It is to seek the truth and relish it, especially when it is inconvenient, even gravely distasteful. I yearn to discomfort those who believe that the rich are not working because they have too little money, the poor are not working because they have too much. Similarly, I yearn to discomfort those who are committed to the prevailing economic doctrine that holds, in metaphor, that if you feed the horse enough oats, some will pass through to the road for the sparrows. I yearn to have as my epitaph: "He Comforted the Afflicted and Afflicted the Comfortable."

John Kenneth Galbraith,
Canadian-born economist, author and educator, served as U.S. ambassador to India

Robert De Giulio
WINNER'S TROPHY

W e are part of the century which
has seen more people killed by war than
in all others combined. Obviously, we don't
know the meaning of life. A vulture
or hyena has more respect for life than
man does.

Rodrigo Poblette
is an artist from Santiago, Chile

Antoine Lecuona
CHILD OF FAMINE, MEIRAM, SUDAN

Jacques Pavlovsky
IRANIAN SOLDIER, IRAQ

Children! I cite, reward, curry and extend them as best I can.

Much is said in this time about The Children. About teenagers. About the problems, the welfare of the young. Much is spoken, many books are written, many "foundations" devised. But rarely has there been, in the whole range of world experience, less *clean* interest in the health and survival of youth.

In many circles, concern for children always and easily comes *after* concern for money, concern for political power, concern for business advancement, concern for drugs and sex, concern for The Look that must be achieved in honor of the next loud luncheon. In other circles, there is concern for children but it is rushed or clipped or coldly departmentalized.

After you've thought *that* over, think of what is happening to thousands of youngsters today. Sexual abuse in some of the respected families, in some of the exquisite mansions. Youngsters chained in basements and sheds. Youngsters jerked off the streets and turned into prostitutes or pornography stars. Youngsters strangled, skinned, sliced, refrigerated, eaten for breakfast or a midnight snack. *(None* of that is absurd symbolism.)

I am proud proud proud when I encounter the many youngsters all over the country who *are* "conducting their blooming in the noise and whip of the whirlwind," since the whirlwind is not going to stop anytime soon.

Does today's society hate and resent children? Many of the young believe that it does, and are responding to galloping alienation by training themselves into a remarkable strength and a canny vigilance.

Self-deprived of childhood innocence, childhood sun? Yes, but *alive*.

Gwendolyn Brooks
is a Pulitzer Prize–winning poet

Being alive in the better sense of the word is the condition of one's pleasant anticipations remaining greater than one's sad regrets. The meaning of life only raises its question when one is sheltered, secure and sleeping and eating well. For when life is threatened and you are holding on to it by any means, there is no mystery that life means that you want to stay alive. And the greatest meaning this can give to you is—not dying before giving life to others. Very much in the same sense comes the question: What does it matter what happens to you when you die? And in the same sense comes the answer: It matters all the days that you live.

J. P. Donleavy,
Irish novelist, is the author of *The Ginger Man*

Why are we here? Because this is as far as we got!

Life itself is the expression of evolution in all its varieties, always from lower to higher, from gross to fine—and sometimes the reverse. Everything that exists is merely matter in motion. In the same way, perfection is always a temporary, relative motion.

Humanity is relative. As a species we have not even managed to extend food, clothing and shelter to our whole selves. (We even have laws against our selves being whole.) We cannot understand our whole beings; our brains are not even half used. What we call thought is presumptuous, at best. We are like the animals on all fours, looking mainly at the ground, unable to obtain the ideas that standing erect should allow.

We are at such a low expression of consciousness that we have not yet seriously studied ourselves. In the main, we do not understand that we are part of the whole of what we call nature.

We are ruled by animal retentionists (our lower selves) who make it illegal or absurd to consider that there is an actual progress or development to human life. They ban history, use the lie of place, rank, status quo, tradition and simple disinformation to try to maintain their place—their power—that cannot be maintained. (The Egyptians called this nonmotion, this evil being, Set.) Hence, our rulers do not worship life itself. They worship the past, the beatification of death, the lust after so-called wealth (a mineral, a low form of earth nature, e.g., gold). In fact, development is circular, yet it traces a rising and twisting motion in which the new torturously replaces the old. Everything is always, and in all ways, motion. Everything is constantly moving at higher, faster, more refined, complex levels of being.

Opposed to Art, violence becomes the real sex of our society ruled by these animal retentionists. This is destruction, the production of the "Art Not," the ecstasy, the happiness or revelation paralleling the screaming of possessed worshipers. Class struggle, the struggles for democracy, for scientific truth, for the production of higher levels of human life are all revolutionary wars.

We will be here as quantitative motion until we reach a state of motion that is qualitative, revolutionary. Then we will be somewhere else!

Amiri Baraka
is an acclaimed American poet and playwright

I am forced to face the inescapable truth. I do not know the meaning of life. I surely do not know it. And what is even more surprising, to be painfully frank, I don't ever even want to know it. Because then I fear I would have to stop soaring and raging with the unquenchable, unspeakable wonder of it all. Oh. Ow! Huh? Gulp! Meow! Woh! Ouch! Mmmm-mmm. ZZZ! Ah. Hmm . . .

Beth Henley
is a Pulitzer Prize–winning playwright

We live life without thinking about life. Each day life provides us with experiences from which we can derive many meanings. Having lost friends and relatives has made me appreciate the value of kinship. Illness has helped me realize the value of health. Having been born a child in the arms of revolution has made me aware of values like freedom and democracy. I have survived foreign occupation, independence, four or five wars; all have greatly affected my perception of life.

When we ask "What is the meaning of life?" we can contemplate the question on two levels: the universal and the individual. On the cosmic level, it makes little sense to imagine why life came to be in the first place. Our answers are merely guesses—stabs at a truth that will always elude us.

On the human level, however, each individual, at birth, has his own "meaning of life." When we are born, we carry within us many motives and desires. We are here to protect life, to survive, to reproduce, to succeed, to become powerful. These desires act as guideposts. One is born with a part of his personal "meaning"; the rest is acquired as we live our lives in relationship to our family and society.

I need not look any further for an answer since the code inside me provides it. Life requests that I survive, reproduce, succeed, work, in order to marry and raise a family. In addition, life asks that I adopt broader objectives such as loyalty to society and, further, to the whole human race. If a person deals with these motives within social limits—within the laws one draws for oneself—then he has accomplished his life's objectives. If he does not adhere to the limits designed by society, and his desires spin out of control, then the desire for survival can lead to murder, the desire to succeed can lead to destroying other people, the love for country can lead to hatred of other nations. On the human level, dealing with life on the basis of normal, social, human principles fulfills, for me, the objective of living a meaningful life.

Naguib Mahfouz,
Egyptian novelist and journalist, won the Nobel Prize for Literature

"What is the meaning of life?" may not be a useful question to ask a child these days because children have no way of experiencing it. Kids grow up on TV and computers and, like adults, are often enclosed within a simulated, artificial reality. They grow up deprived of contact with organic nature. I don't think we can ask what the meaning of life is until we reintegrate ourselves into living relationships.

I remember going to the circus a few years ago. I was having a good time until they started the elephant act. They had an elephant dressed up in a little apron and hat and made it do a handstand on a little drum. All of a sudden, I was embarrassed—for myself and for everyone there. I was ashamed of our species for having taken this gorgeous, sentient creature and reducing it to an entertaining plaything.

Part of life's meaning comes in not being afraid to experience it on its own terms. We are constantly trying to remake and manipulate life so that it conforms to our image of what we would like it to be. In the process, we lose life's essence. If we were to accept life on its own terms and allow other creatures to experience the fullness of their beings, we could add to the enrichment of all life.

Jeremy Rifkin,
lecturer and author, is an antibiotechnology activist

Every human being has asked, upon becoming aware of his existence: Whence do we come? Where do we go? Ever since man has gained awareness of eternity, he has been pondering the end of endlessness. Forever, human beings will continue to pose an endless string of questions.

In his *Iliad,* Homer says that of all creatures, human beings suffer most because they are the only species conscious of death. We are ever asking: What is eternity? Does it end? If so, where? And why do we die?

These unbearable thoughts have always weighed heavily upon mankind. And because man could not find answers, he created myths, gods, saints and imaginary worlds, in which he found relief from the difficulties of life, from death and endless darkness, carnage, war, earthquakes, disasters and want. Many an epic, from *Gilgamesh* to the *Odyssey,* from the *Iliad* to *Manas* to *Kalevala,* has addressed the quest for eternal life. Epics can be described, in a way, as challenges to death. Such tales have also dwelt upon another theme: that it is good to have come into the world, good to exist against death, against nature's cruelty, against the questions "What if we had not existed at all?" and "What is the meaning of life?"

In the face of suffering, crisis and hopelessness, and as a way to understand the meaning of life, human beings continue to exhibit an unbelievable joie de vivre. As they gain consciousness about life, this joy increases along with their sense of attachment to their existence. When they fail in this effort, they create dreamworlds in which they seek refuge. And, in the process of spinning myths, a new concept emerges: If we did not exist, there would be no universe at all—an idea that comforts the mind and makes life easier. But always, underneath, lurks mankind's primary worry: What is the nature of eternal existence?

We may think, at certain stages, that we have solved these mysteries. Yet the ages will pile new mysteries upon the old until, one day, we will reach the conclusion, perhaps, that the meaning of life lies in humankind's creative power. In the meantime, humanity will believe, at all costs, that even if existence is followed by death, even if existence is a process of emerging from one kind of darkness only to enter another, life itself, and the good fortune of having been born in the first place, are well worth celebrating in glowing songs and epics.

Yashar Kemal,
of Kurdish descent, is Turkey's preeminent novelist

In ancient times, "Why are we here?" was an inquiry that occupied an important place in the mind of mankind. With the coming of the industrial revolution, however, man became preoccupied with the material sciences and began to lose touch with his inner self.

Our souls are like streams that can never rest until they once again mingle with the Infinite sea. Until that time comes, we meander, trying new lines of least resistance. At times the stream of life seems shallow, at other times deep, sometimes dark and murky, sometimes pure and crystal clear. At times we enter lakes of the spirit that are so large and still that they deceive us into thinking we have reached the ocean of the Infinite. Sometimes we are lured into swamps of uncertainty, trapped in tidal pools from which we fear we may never escape. From lifetime to lifetime the stream goes on, searching, suffering, pursuing the Infinite reunion.

A balance existed between the endless sharing of the Creator and the endless receiving of His creations—the souls of man. This condition of unity might have gone on forever. But the souls of man felt ashamed at the one-sidedness of their relationship with the Creator. This condition, which results from receiving that which is not earned, is defined in Kabbalistic terms as Bread of Shame. Thus, the Creator withdrew so that the Infinite could give birth to the finite. That moment of divine conception, known to Kabbalists as the Thought of Creation, and to scientists as the big bang, was the root of Creation, the source from which the universe expanded, complete with all its phases and diversity, physical and meta-physical, as it was, is and forever will be.

We are here to earn the beneficence of the Creator. This is a process sometimes too difficult to accomplish in one lifetime, but fortunately we are provided with as many lifetimes as necessary. The desire for unification is nourished by the *Zohar*, written by Rabbi Shimon Bar Yohai some 2,000 years ago, containing all of the truths of the nature of existence and our function in it. Written in Aramaic, the book has the power to impress the reader with positive energy simply by scanning its letters. The Kabbalah, which many believe to be the secret code that governs the universe, provides the security shield mankind presently requires to sustain and protect itself from the chaos and misfortune that are now so prevalent.

Philip Berg,
rabbi, is dean and director of the International Research Centre of Kabbalah

Hiroji Kubota
BURMESE MONKS PRAYING BEFORE A GILDED BOULDER

Ortega y Gasset writes about the monkey that looks in every direction and falls asleep. We, on the other hand, have the ability to focus and to bring the searchlight onto what we know. If we tune in to our core, our center, our roots, if we are fortunate, we can contribute something, through passion and discipline, to the record of what has been. We are born and we die. We are born and we die. By understanding our interrelatedness to the chain gang of life, meaning comes.

Nancy Graves

is an American painter, sculptor, filmmaker, and costume and set designer

We are created by God for union with Himself. That's really what Christian creeds espouse. That's really the meaning of heaven too: fulfillment, wholeness. The whole point and purpose of the Christian faith resides in its community. Christianity is not isolationist. You are part of the body of Christ, the family of God. The Church is community. Community is being part of a common life, being the hands and feet and voice of the Christ Who is our Master. Christ did say: Though no man has seen God, we have to learn how to love God through loving one another.

I once met a remarkable Native American from Canada at an interfaith conference I hosted for the World Council of Churches. Over the course of demonstrating how his belief was tied into the earth and the mountains and the streams, it seemed that the symbolism of his faith was almost identical to the Catholic symbolism. When he preached, he held a staff. Instead of incense, he used a smoking flax burned in a bowl. It became apparent that the further we engage in a proper dialogue between faiths, the more we realize we have in common.

Trevor Huddleston,

former Anglican Archbishop of the Indian Ocean, CR, is president of the Anti-Apartheid Movement in Britain and chairman of the Defense and Aid Fund for Southern Africa

Mark Greenberg
Meditation, Buddha Hall,
Rajneeshpuram, Oregon

166

Susie Fitzhugh
AMISH GIRLS AT PLAY, GORMAN, MARYLAND

A s a child I fantasized about life in a dreamland. Imagination, Innocence and Inspiration—the three I's—were the passwords to opening the gate to this land.

Today I still dream about life. These dreams give me hope and are the main spiritual source of energy for my life. What do I dream about? Of many, many things: things I wish would happen, things I wish would not happen and, most importantly, things I feel. These I cannot explain with words.

Music has various meanings to various people. For me, it is a means to communicate with myself and with others from the heart, without words. It is a communication, or rather a conversation, of our hearts and of our feelings. As long as I have my music I can keep dreaming and live my life. And I live my life to dream.

Midori,
20-year-old Japanese violin virtuoso, made her U.S. debut at age nine

Bill Foley
SISTERS ON A GARBAGE MOUNTAIN, CAIRO

167

There's something to learn from everything, even misfortune, or perhaps especially misfortune. I was shipwrecked and lost my boat, which I loved dearly. A fisherman named Juan saved me and let me stay in his storage shack at the beach until I could salvage my boat. One day he told me about his own accident. He was out at sea with a full boat of fish when the motor broke. Another fisherman loaded all the fish onto his boat and took it to the harbor. Juan told the fisherman to keep the fish, since they would have been lost without his help. But the fisherman said no, keep them, they're yours. So Juan asked what he could do to thank the man for his help. And the fisherman said, "By helping the next man you see in trouble you'll be thanking me."

I don't believe in the law of karma, which maintains your good and bad deeds are recorded in a spiritual bank account. I think if you do poorly in one life, you simply repeat that stage, like you would a grade in school. We're here to learn, not to be punished.

Carlos Carvalo
is a casino croupier in Montevideo, Uruguay

Laundry has always been my favorite thing to do. It reminds me a little of life—sometimes soiled, sometimes blown about. But when I hang sheets and watch them blow gently in the breeze, clean and sweet-smelling, the memories and scents of yesteryear flow back and wash away all bitterness, sadness and anger. Inside myself, all's right with me and the world. A clean slate, a fresh sheet, a new page in the book of life.

Beverly Ann Smith
is a wife, mother of four, and grandmother, living in Mantua, New Jersey

Always, we have to make our mind pure, not guilty. When we have full peace in our heart, we have peace in life. When we read the Bible and follow it pure, what bad do you have? Nothing. Always restful heart, happy feeling. Wherever you go, you have the chance to meet nice people because you did nice. Wherever there are people, there are nice people.

Everyone has a purpose. They have to solve it for themselves. Always, I'm here in my office. This is like concrete in my mind. If I'm here, I'm very happy. I am here, I go home, see some news, then to my bed. I'm back here at 7:30. I like typing. I like my job. It's my character. Always my life is my work. My work is my life. From the time I was a baby, I like it. When you have a clean bed, a pillow to put your head on, clean water and nice fresh bread, this is the best life. Right? In the morning, a piece of bread. That's enough with a cup of tea, and cheese. You cannot have more. Our Father Who art in heaven, give us this day our daily bread. It is a meaning.

I don't like to travel. The chair in my office I like. Me marry? Eeee, never. My business is my marriage. What for, marriage? Your health is your marriage. Your health is your children. Your health is your life. If you're healthy, you live happy. Me, no regret. For what? I enjoy being alone. This is life. Always, we say, this is life.

Vicky Khano,
born in Jerusalem, is a Palestinian travel agent living in Amman, Jordan

Whatever I want becomes what life is about. My life is absolutely complete now that I have two grandchildren. I can't say what's missing. You're always searching, searching. Sometimes you're not even sure what for. My grandchildren, spicy food and going on holidays give meaning to my life.

Raja Nor Jasmin
is a princess and restaurateur in Kuala Lumpur, Malaysia

You can be as sad as you want or as happy as you want. It's totally up to you. We Cajuns—all our misery, we going to make some happiness out of it, why not? Nobody has ever given me a reason why not to be happy. The onliest way to live is to enjoy, giving an honest day's work for an honest day's pay, and then comes that weekend. That's why we say joie de vivre—just enjoy the damn old thing. I think the world has missed being born a Cajun.

It might have been six or eight years back. I'm sitting reading the Bible, and it said: Look at the birds, who feeds them? I was drinking an excellent cup of coffee, watching a bird eating in the yard, and right then it dawned on me. I said, "You know, there's a point to this. Who feeds the birds if there's not a higher power? What the hell you worried about? You can't control anything if you try." You are born to die, period. And no man ever escaped that but one. Me and you have no control over our destiny so we must go enjoy life. Any human can fall in a rut and you can't get out and, oh, it's awful. And there will come a time when you remember: Saturday afternoon with pots of coffee and French music on television, Mama dancing on the floor by herself. That's what this life is all about. Oh, man, that was joyous times.

Mike Morris,
of New Iberia, Louisiana, is a chili cook and a hot sauce sales representative

John Loengard
TAKING A NAP IN THE SUMMERHOUSE

I write this from the Pottsville prison. Yards from here, the Molly Maguires were hanged in 1877 for their militancy in protesting working conditions in Pennsylvania's mines. I wonder what they thought about life in their final moments.

In jail, separated from family, friends and everyday pressures, it is easier to contemplate life. I am here because I believe that the values placed on lives of different sorts are inequitable, and that my own life provides opportunities to change the equation.

Specifically, I am here, in this cell, because I found myself unwilling to watch quietly as pigeons—bewildered by gunfire and exhausted from lack of food and water—had their wings and legs shot off. All in sport. Almost 100 of us ran onto the shooting field. We opened trap boxes to set free the living targets. Then we lay down to stop the gunners' fire.

As I ran, I repeated Winston Churchill's words "Never give in, never, never, never, never." To me, the war our "civilized" species wages against all the others, and our enslavement and slaughter of animals for nothing more than a fashion statement, a fleeting taste or an amusement, is no less immoral than other acts of unbridled aggression and prejudice now condemned by history.

Outside my cell, starlings are nesting in the high stone wall. Iridescent flecks of green and gold sparkle from their perfect wings. Watching them, I know that animal liberation will come, for all life is precious, no matter how tiny or odd or puzzling its form.

Ingrid Newkirk,
animal rights activist, is the national director of People for the Ethical Treatment of Animals

Charles Mason
ESKIMOS COMFORTING TRAPPED GRAY WHALE, BARROW, ALASKA

Helen Chadwick
Ego Geometria Sum: The Labors I Birth

172

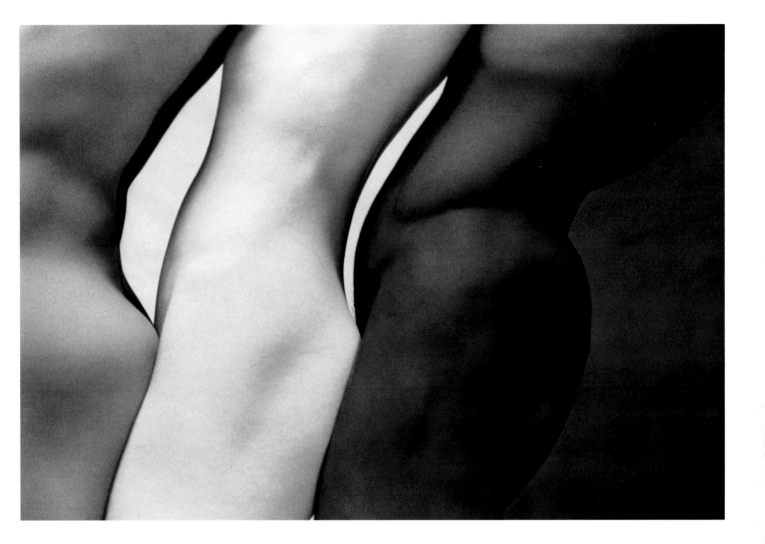

Eikoh Hosoe
EMBRACE #60

Ramón Masats
SEMINARY, MADRID

Rome fell, according to historian Lewis Mumford, not through political or economic or military ineptitude. Rome collapsed through "a leeching away of meaning and a loss of faith." Mumford might just as well have been speaking about our culture—a society afflicted by cynicism, selfishness and an erosion of civility, a society that has lost faith in its leaders and institutions and hungers for a greater sense of human connectedness.

It is no coincidence, I submit, that ours is a society fixated on the externals. We are preoccupied with the pursuit of bottom lines, consumption, careerism—and winning. We pursue a vision of human salvation through "progress," one of the most powerful unifying myths of our 20th century life. We place our faith in what we can see, touch and hear, and instinctively grasp for numbers to understand the world. We remain suspicious of the unquantifiable, the intuitive, the mysterious.

Yet a culture that becomes a stranger to its own inner needs—which *are,* for better or worse, unquantifiable, intuitive and mysterious—is a culture that has lost touch with the best in its humanity, its sense of shared moral values, its ethics, creativity, passion, wonder and joy.

Could it be that, individually and collectively, we are failing to address one of our most basic human needs—the exploration of our mysterious inner life?

However wondrous, useful, ingenious and economically profitable the fruits of "progress," none of them satisfy the needs that relate to the inner life, where the capacities for awe, wonder and mystery abide and seek nourishment. Our failure to look within ourselves is directly related to our knowing destruction of the life-sustaining capacities of the planet. The logging of ancient forests, the frequent oil spills at sea, the perpetual creation of garbage, the extinction of 10,000 species per year—the whole litany of slow-motion environmental catastrophes from acid rain to the ozone layer to global warming—are acts of a society that has lost its sense of identity as a mortal, endangered species on a fragile little planet in a vast cosmos. How else could a society show such little regard for posterity and commonweal, and engage in such flagrant acts of psychic self-mutilation?

The hunger in the American psyche for connectedness and spiritual renewal is not confined to our nation. It extends to the peoples of third-world nations, many of whom have been made to feel estranged—by progress and politics, by poverty and famine—from the spiritual world their ancestors held dear. It extends also to the Soviet Union and Eastern Europe, where the suppression of the spirit has been deliberate for decades. This is, in fact, a global hunger.

Vaclav Havel, Czechoslovakia's dissident-turned-President, points out that the most dangerous walls are not political or military boundaries but, as he puts it, "the walls that mutually divide individual people and that divide our own souls." As a corrective, Havel announced that his presidential agenda would be "to bring spirituality, moral responsibility, humaneness and humility into politics and, in that respect, to make clear that there is something higher above us."

Why has no American politician dared to speak similarly, let alone adopt such a platform? How surprised would they be to learn that most Americans would welcome a call to make commitments to higher values, to bring spirituality, moral responsibility, humaneness and humility into politics?

Too squeamish to confront these issues, mainstream secular culture has instead surrendered this territory to those on the fringes—the revivalists, the New Age swamis, the self-help ego boosters, the religious right. This has been a mistake. The desire to lead a more purposeful life, to search for ultimate meanings, is a central theme of human experience.

We need to reclaim this domain as a legitimate and urgent cultural concern. In so doing, we must respect each other's faiths, of course. And let us stand by the traditional First Amendment wall that separates church and state. But let us not be so skittish or parochial as to think that one of the great human imperatives—the rediscovery and reinvention of a common spiritual life in our desolate modern age—can or should be suppressed. If we think of our nation's diverse religions as uniquely different streams that each feed into a single thousand-mile river—a river of humanity—can we agree to discuss that river openly and freely, as a common source of values that nurtures all of our spiritual traditions?

This spiritual urge is undeniable. From the beginning of human history, we have been embarked on a search for transcendent meaning. It is as if we were genetically coded to believe that there is a greater force and mystery framing our lives. Which is why the next great improvement in the human condition will occur not through a millennial faith in technology but by uncovering a new, more spiritually satisfying notion of "progress," one that requires a vertical leap of faith, a leap in our inner development. The answer is not to ignore these issues in schools and other institutions. It is to fling open the doors—and find new ways of learning more about our myriad values and spiritual traditions in order to realize what we all hold in common as a species.

Norman Lear,

television producer, writer and director, created *All in the Family* and is a founder of the civil rights organization People for the American Way

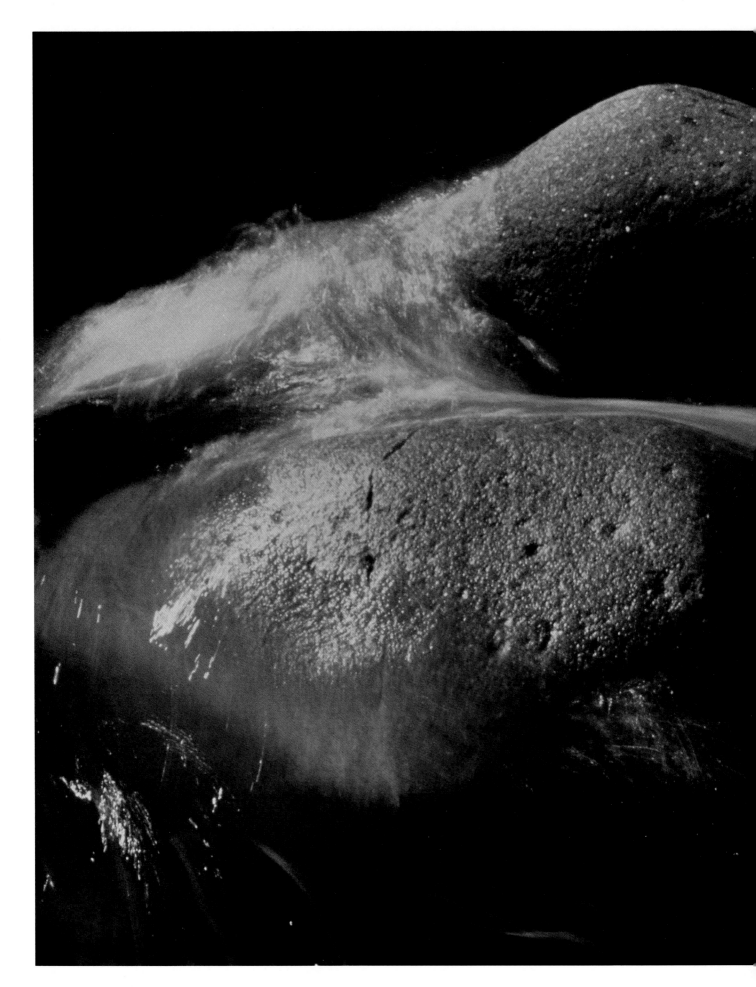

When I die, I want to be buried, not in a wooden casket, but nude, standing up, close to the surface of the earth, so that I can change into a butterfly or I can give life to a flower.

Life is love. And sexuality, a vital part of life, should emerge freely in every individual. Each of us should explore sexuality as effortlessly as a bee pollinates a flower.

I've never felt guilt or shame in my sexual life. I have always tried to share this beautiful freedom with all people. Part of my mission in life is to promote sexual liberty without any form of censorship.

Curiosity, sexual and otherwise, is what makes life interesting.

Cicciolina,
adult film star, performance artist and advocate of sexual freedom, is a deputy in the Italian parliament

Heinz Teufel
MOTHER EARTH

Life is a mother and child, suffering, falling, getting up, laughing, crying, wiping away the tears. You can't live without suffering, but you can't let that stop your life.

Life is never what you expect. When I was 24 and my older daughter was five, I learned she was retarded. All my hopes and dreams crashed to the floor. I was nearly paralyzed by the pain of knowing that she would suffer and that I was powerless to help. The future filled me with fear.

She was so innocent, and I was so afraid of what she would suffer. I had to work extra to pay for her instruction. It was all I could do to meet her special needs while I was alive. Who would take care of her after I died? And as for my younger daughter, I never felt I gave her as much as she deserved either.

My daughters are now 28 and 31, and they are my life's greatest joy. They have become wonderful human beings. My older daughter is independent and responsible. She is a very special person and loved by many; she makes me happier each day. I know she'll be able to take care of herself when I'm no longer here. I never hoped for such a reward, I never dreamed I could die in peace.

My life has been the life of my daughters. Most of my years have already passed and there's little time to do anything about it. But I guess as long as I'm alive, there's time. I've just started learning tailoring and dressmaking and it's a good feeling to do something simply because you want to.

Concepción Méndez,
a laundress, lives in Montevideo, Uruguay

Abigail Heyman
WEDDING RECEPTION

Like my father and grandfather, I've worked all my life on the Nile. These boats have been here since the pharaohs.

The water talks to me. It says, "My love, where are you?" The Nile is the source, the soul of the people. It spreads so far down. The Nile has taught me patience. I spend hours and hours on my own. It has taught me to be caring. Sometimes the wind is so strong I have to protect my boat and the people on my boat. Look at that fisherman with his wife and kids. All their time is spent on that boat. His wife goes to shore only to buy their vegetables. These are people who like peacefulness. There are problems out there, like in the suburbs—too much human contact creates problems. Living on the Nile, I'm better off. No cars, no beatings. If something is upsetting, come and watch the Nile. You'll be in a great state of mind. Its power comes from its peacefulness.

Life is happiness. When I'm happy at work and my wife is satisfied, this is happiness. If she needs a galabia, I'll go and get her one before she even asks. I love my wife. She's been living with me 50 years. There hasn't been a day when we really quarreled. Some men commit suicide because their wives are really unbearable. Yes, it's true, women kill themselves, but a man will throw himself into the Nile because he hasn't enough money to support his wife or feed the children. Some people with lots of money have lots of problems. I prefer to be a happy man, not owning a piaster, going into my house and finding a caring wife.

Our purpose is to marry and have kids and teach them how to get away from problems.

Ahmed Ibrahim el Degui,
also known as Dok-Dok, sails feluccas down the Nile

Annie Leibovitz
SAMUEL AND MARILYN LEIBOVITZ, SILVER SPRING, MARYLAND

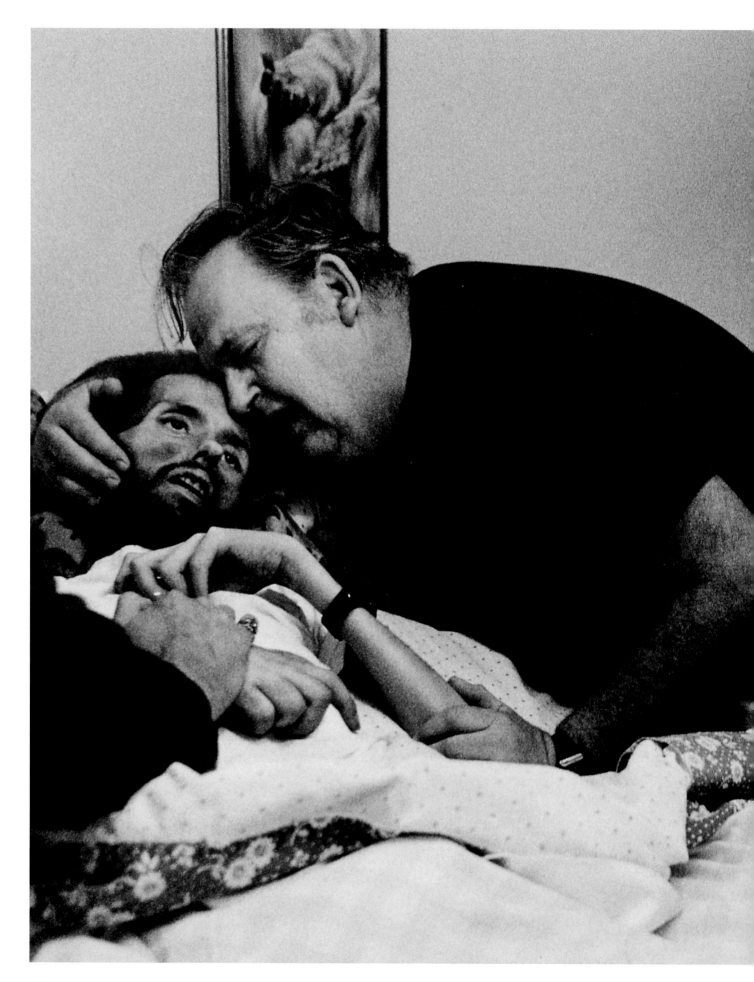

180

I have always liked the dark side of the human soul and have been attracted by all sorts of subcultures. I try not to evaluate people, saying this person or that person is bad. I try to notice, very quickly, what is good in others. If I didn't, I would go crazy. If you took an objective look at the people I work with, you'd say they're nobody. But it's not true. They have plenty of wonderful qualities.

Man, by nature, is rather dark, I think. The art of living is the art of getting out of the darkness. On your way you meet lots of people who are able to disperse lots of darkness; you have to find the rare ones who specialize in light. We must work on creating light—tolerance for others, maximum respect and reduction of human fears. I know what people need. They need love. Human beings should be good and brave. Everybody should be able to love—and for nothing. My point in life is giving myself to others. Ten years ago I only wanted to get people off their dependencies. Now, there is something else driving me. I want to be shoulder to shoulder with the dying. I think they have a right to be who they are. I tell them, "Each of us should decide his or her own death. You can be afraid of it or strive to achieve it. Maybe you would like to choose something besides death. But, if not, I'm going to be with you until the end." I am someone standing on a sea of trouble, trying to build bridges so unhappy people can cross to the other side. I am in a hurry. Unfortunately, I don't think I will live long. I have cancer of the throat. In a way, it may be cruel: I may lose something very important to me, my voice, which is my energy. People say they like the way I talk. I don't know why God wants my death. I would like to ask Him myself. He should know that I am needed here. I am doing what he used to be doing, helping the needy and the sick. Maybe if God reads this book, he will change his mind.

Marek Kotanski,
peace and human rights activist, has set up shelters in Poland for substance abusers, the homeless and people with AIDS

Therese Frare
DAVID KIRBY SUCCUMBS TO AIDS, COLUMBUS, OHIO

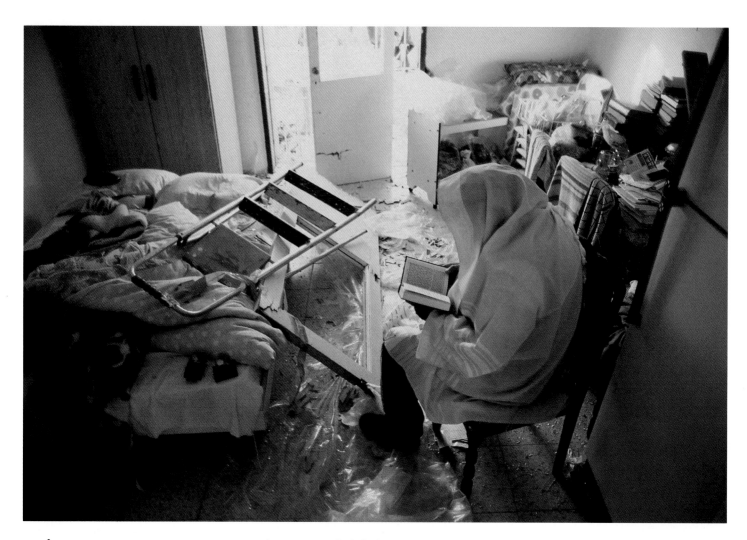

David H. Wells
SCUD ATTACK AFTERMATH, TEL AVIV

A man becomes a monk to try to save his soul, grow close to God and consecrate a relationship with the Almighty. Some people might say it's a selfish existence, but it's not. You cannot love if you are selfish, and growing close to God is an act of love.

Religion is dealing not with mechanics but with moral values, spiritual truths that we learn through divine revelation. In magic you say the formula and take three steps to the left, four to the right and throw something over your shoulder. Magic makes nice movies, like *Star Wars* or *E.T.*, but spaceships don't take you to God. You go to God through considerable exercise of patience, by keeping your mouth shut when you want to talk.

In the fourth century, the theologian St. Athanasius said something to the effect that the meaning of life is for us to become by grace what God is by nature. The pilgrimage is the same for everybody, monk or not: from less virtue to more, from lack of holiness to growth of holiness.

Monk N
(who wishes to remain anonymous)
is an Eastern Orthodox cleric in Jerusalem

David Hume Kennerly
MEMORIAL FOR EARTHQUAKE
VICTIMS, ARMENIA

Robin Moyer
AFGHAN SCHOOL

I let loose a thousand baby turtles once, hoping one of them might live to be a 40-year-old. They estimate that only one in a thousand of these turtles survives.

If you give some people self-esteem and tools to survive, that's what it's all about. I remember Paul, a little boy I was teaching. He was very intelligent, but his mom and dad didn't have the same priorities he had about education. I started reading the works of Roald Dahl to the class, and Paul got hooked. Well, one Friday I told the class, "On Saturday night Roald Dahl is going to be interviewed on television. If you remember, watch it." Of course, six-year-olds don't remember what day it is most of the time. But on Monday morning this little guy came in and said, "Mrs. Walpole, I watched that interview. Roald Dahl talked about all the values of life and how people are too busy and haven't got time to stop and think and talk and read stories. He talked about the books he's written, and you've read most of them to us. He talked about how reading can light people's spark." And then Paul said, "You know what? You lit my spark." And I sort of got all goosey. You can almost hear the hair rise on your arms when children say things like that. You think, "Perhaps there's some purpose in my being here."

I suppose it's like the little turtles. If we can get one to survive out of all those thousands, maybe it's worth the bother.

Dorothy Walpole
teaches grade school in Newcastle, Australia

T he meaning of life? It is life itself! Does the Lord not say, If I place life and death before you, blessing and curse, you will choose life? How could a child of the Warsaw ghetto have been able to choose anything other than life? With jubilation, of course. Also with the dreams that life carries along: justice, solidarity, respect for others.

I have fought to make that life a reality. But can one trap the moon in a pail of water? The Jews of Chelm, who considered themselves the cleverest people in the world, thought they could do it. Each evening they waited until the moon was reflected in their cherished bucket. Then they slapped down the cover. But, alas, the moon was never there the next morning.

Am I like these clever ones of Chelm? Am I going to attempt this folly each and every morning? But of course. If life has a meaning, it is certainly to try, every day, to realize one's dreams. Ultimately, everything moves. Event follows event. Who knows if, one day, it will not be possible to trap the moon in a pail of water? I would love to be on hand the day that dream comes true.

Marek Halter,
storyteller, novelist and human rights activist, is president of the French University in Moscow

I spent nearly all my life surrounded by lies—as a youth in fascist Italy, then in an authoritarian Hungary where lying was prevalent, followed by Germany's wartime occupation, then 45 years of Communism. So you can't really be astonished if I tell you I am not religious. But I have learned to guide my life by the Ten Commandments. I think they form the line to which you have to adjust your life. You can't say, "Well, I'll accept nine, but not the one that isn't really convenient at certain moments." For me, they are absolute laws.

The main endeavor in my life has been the struggle for truth. If, at the end of my life, one would ask me, "What do you consider your main achievement?" I would answer, "I have three children and eight grandchildren—and none of them is lying." They are common people, of course. Not extraordinary. But that is something. In some way I feel I have achieved eternity. That is how we live on after dying. If I can transmit what I have learned to my children, and my children to theirs, I feel my life has a meaning.

Miklós Vásárhelyi,
member of the Hungarian parliament, formerly imprisoned for his opposition to the Communist regime, is the sole survivor of the revolutionary government suppressed by the Soviets in 1956

G eorge Thomas, former Speaker of the House of Commons, was ill. I had been told, in fact, that he was dying. So I went to sit with him in the hospital. Well, I've never had an experience like it in my life. He was a man who had no fear of death at all. He knew he was going to join his Maker, knew there was a God, and I was stunned by the absolute clarity of his belief. When you're about to die, you're at your most honest and revealing. His honesty and attitude staggered me.

Two years down the line, of course, he's still here, as right as rain. I saw him the other day on the House of Commons terrace. And that made me wonder even more. He'd had a word with the Maker, and the Maker said, "You had better stay a while longer."

Does this make me question what we're supposed to do with our lives? All I can say is: Heaven knows why we're here. I literally mean that. It's so easy to say "Do your best" and all that drivel. I can't believe we're all set out with a purpose. But I do think most of us can do better than we believe; few of us actually achieve what we are capable of. Again and again, especially in times of adversity, people like George Thomas—or the young, who are particularly enthusiastic in their feelings for those in trouble—manage to rise beyond their dreams. We should all realize we can do things we would never dream possible and aspire to achieve those dreams.

Jeffrey Archer,
suspense writer, was deputy chairman of the Conservative Party and the youngest member ever elected to Britain's House of Commons

Masatoshi Naito
OLD WOMEN IN A BURST, JAPAN

I must tell you a story. I'm a Muslim. And I once went to the U.S. and met this Christian couple there. They brought me to church, and afterward their pastor came to my recording studio. In any case, we ended up going everywhere together, night and day. They even baptized me. I would never have believed that there were people like that, people ready to sacrifice all for love. And I realized paradise has many gates, that there are Muslims who go to paradise just as there are Christians who go to paradise. Lead a correct life, love others—and I'll see you in paradise.

Salif Keita
is an internationally renowned performer, singer and composer from Mali

Arlene Gottfried
SELWYN RAWLS AND THE ETERNAL LIGHT
COMMUNITY SINGERS, HARLEM

Observations of distant galaxies have produced growing and provocative evidence for a startling idea: Our universe was just one "bubble" in a great fountain of bubble universes springing from the big bang, which created all reality. Each universe has its own distinct physical laws and constants. There will be those with but one gigantic star; others will have no stars at all and will exist in eternal darkness. Ours is one born, perhaps by chance, with just the right laws and constants to have made complicated molecules possible. And, after billions of years, those molecules have developed into ever more sophisticated living structures that we have evolved into creatures conscious of our universe, able to manipulate it in massive ways. We can contemplate and cherish our universe only because it has been precisely optimized to have made living things, such as us, possible.

Life, by definition, probably exists in many forms in many places in our universe. It is arrogance to think that the earthbound have any true grasp of the complex meaning, or meanings, of life; we have not yet gathered all the data. Our own significance, our ultimate potential and our ensemble of possible destinies will be understood only by finding and studying the other intelligent creatures of space. Thus, a prime task for us is to seek these other intelligent civilizations and join them in shared knowledge. We now have the means to do so, and if we are as noble as we think, we will proceed vigorously with this enterprise.

Frank Drake,

president of the SETI (Search for Extraterrestrial Intelligence) Institute, is an astrophysicist

Are we alone in the universe? This is perhaps the question most frequently asked of astronomers. My own attitude toward this issue inevitably influences my views on the meaning of life.

I was brought up in the early years of the century, when prevailing scientific wisdom that since Earth and the planets orbiting the Sun were a system unique in all the universe, life on Earth was itself unique. As our ideas about the life history of stars developed, this theory of uniqueness was discarded. Most astronomers would now agree that the occurrence of planetary systems around stars must be a natural consequence of the evolution of stars from the primeval material of the universe. But until 1991 there was no observational evidence to support this view. That year astronomers at England's Jodrell Bank laboratories published evidence that they had discovered a planet orbiting a star far away in the Milky Way.

Eugene A. Cernan/NASA
PANORAMA AT THE LUNAR CRATER CAMELOT

In fact, theory and observation are now in harmony. Our solar system is not unique, and we must accept the view that planets orbit stars elsewhere in the universe. That discovery has settled one of science's great mysteries, but it does not answer the vital question of whether life has evolved in any of these remote planetary systems. Many astronomers are so convinced that the answer must be positive that they are spending large sums, and most of their careers, in search of signals from extraterrestrial civilizations. My own opinion remains conservative. The conditions that have allowed Earth to support life's evolution have been delicately balanced over four billion years. It remains an act of faith, unsupported by scientific evidence, that similar conditions have existed on planets elsewhere in the universe.

Until such direct evidence is obtained, I prefer to believe in the uniqueness of life on Earth—an evolutionary event without cosmic precedent, a singular event to be treasured and preserved from the many material forces that sometimes seem destined to destroy us.

Sir Bernard Lovell,
astronomer, pioneered the field of radio astronomy and helped develop modern radar

$$M_\oplus > e^3 m_e^{\frac{3}{2}}/G^{\frac{3}{2}} m_p^{\frac{7}{2}} \sim 4 \times 10^{25}\, g$$

A man who asks "Why are we here?" is addressing a universal issue, yet he expects a reasonable, logical, comprehensible answer. He demands that his answer conform to logic, for man's understanding proceeds only in logical forms. This requirement to conform to logic, however, strongly restricts the formal laws that govern the universe. Very few universal laws satisfy the requirement that they be inherently logical.

The laws of the universe govern everything. Without them a man wouldn't even be capable of asking "Why are we here?" But those laws, having been already uniquely selected and predetermined, leave no room for a further "free choice" or for a deeper, overarching "reason" outside of those laws.

Logically, the ultimate answer to the question "Why are we here?" *should* be: "Because the laws of the universe determined that we are here." But this assumes that the laws, like the man asking the question, are themselves somehow governed by logic. In effect, asking the question places constructs upon the universe to which it cannot conform.

If there exists an ultimate answer as to why we are here, it is: "We are here to raise the question 'Why are we here?'"

Fang Lizhi,
physicist and dissident, now in exile in America, helped lead China's democracy movement in 1989, taking refuge in the U.S. embassy during the Tiananmen Square incident

189

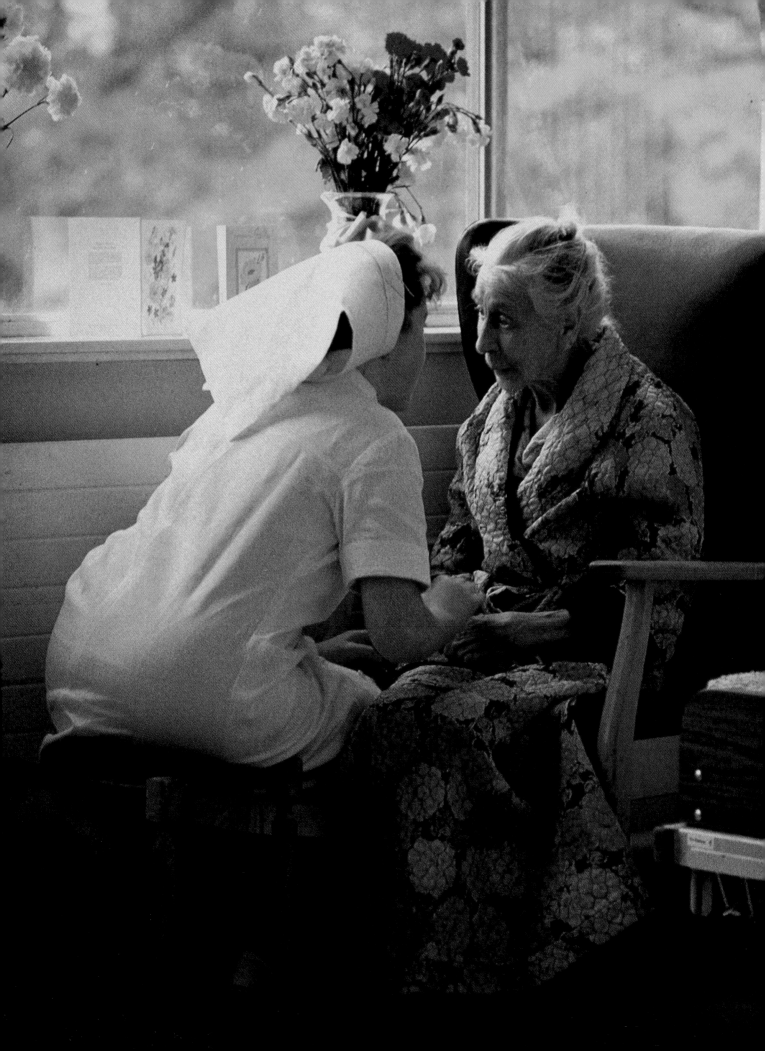

I believe that you only pass through this world one time so don't defer this chance—and thank goodness you can do works of kindness and show a human being beauty. I look around myself and try to figure out what it is I can do, what I can give back, and that gives my life purpose.

Many times I have to be with babies whose mothers were on crack and, although they know they're dying when they go, they're so quiet and just drift off. But the further people get from babyhood, the more scared they are of dying. I'll stay with an adult patient who is dying, and he'll be in turmoil about dying, even when he's nearly comatose. I'll put my hand on his chest and feel all his rage and fury and fight, just like a volcano. He's making it so difficult to die when dying is the normal conclusion of his illness and he has already fought so hard. I'll put my hands in his hand and stroke his brow and calmly whisper, "It's all right."

But don't get me wrong. Dying is no fun. I've had 15 major operations. I've been on the brink of life and death many times. I've been to hell and back, materially, financially, physically, and I know that death holds no frills.

Every life has a purpose, and this is the purpose of mine. I have a Ph.D. in pain and loneliness and being penniless, but I can use that for people in the same position to let them know life goes on. If they're sick, I tell them they can fight. If they're poor, I let them know they can do something and be someone regardless of their situation. I just feel that I am your friend, and as a nurse and a person who has been a patient many times, I am your information center, and I am always someone you can communicate with and not worry about being judged.

Fanniedell Peeples
is a nurse, social worker and
health-care advocate in Detroit, Michigan

For me, life is very clear. There are only two kinds of man in the world: the oppressed and the oppressor. There is no neutral. My philosophy is: You can measure your life's worth by how many people you serve. If you work for your husband, you work for a single individual. If you work for your family, you are valued by that family. If you work for a community or society, you are precious to them.

All must work for their fellow human beings. Without that, the meaning of life is not fulfilled. Working for other people is the value of life.

How many people are you working for?

Aye Saung
is a resistance leader in the antigovernment
Democratic Alliance of Burma

I can tell a lot about people by touching them and examining their bones. Everybody has certain characteristics. Older bodies are completely different than younger ones. They are like puppets; their arms and legs have a life of their own. But giving a massage isn't just about rubbing down bodies. You are also massaging the soul. When people come to me, they pour out their problems. Part of my job is in my lips. I give advice and sometimes prescribe natural treatments. If there were 200 thermal bathhouses in Hungary, our troubles would be solved.

To give. To give to my family and then to my customers. This is the only thing that matters. Giving is the most important thing in life, along with kindness and patience. People need attention. When a client comes in and is angry and has problems, I want her to leave feeling completely differently.

When I die I want to know that it was worth living, that I served others well.

Jánosné Gyönki
is a masseuse at a thermal bathhouse
in Budapest, Hungary

When I was nine years old, I was living in East Harlem and I became sick with rheumatic fever and was hospitalized for a year. That experience transformed me. It exposed me to the larger world, to people outside my neighborhood, to people involved in health care in particular. I had also learned how valuable it is to break down cultural barriers. I had gratitude toward the doctors and nurses who I felt had saved my life. And I had a dream of becoming a doctor and helping people as I had been helped. My illness was a kind of blessing. If I hadn't gotten sick I may have ended up in jail. Most of my friends went to jail. They became drug addicts or criminals. In fact, most of them are dead.

Knowing how I could have ended up, I developed a philosophy, a commitment to influence society in a positive way. If there's any spiritual vision I have, that's it. We are here to try to make people grow stronger and more self-reliant, even when it means submerging our own egos. In developing oneself, there should always be some sense of community, some service orientation to it.

As a psychiatrist, I run into people socially and clinically who are obsessed with acquisition. I find that their desire for a better house or their competition with one another for more and more goods just feeds on itself and doesn't fulfill them. That's an empty way to live. I feel that giving is important for sustaining people spiritually, but receiving is not.

Alvin Poussaint,
Harvard professor of psychiatry, developed
the "aggression-rage" theory, which describes
the effect of racism on the black psyche

Nick Kelsh
DUBLIN NURSE

The meaning of life is having the
boys chase me, having the other kids be nice
and having fun.

Charlotte Jones
is the three-year-old daughter
of singer-songwriter Rickie Lee Jones

Wes Wilson
HAS BOW, NEEDS BELT

Dennis Brack
THE DANCERS, NATIONAL GALLERY
OF ART, WASHINGTON, D.C.

(Overleaf)
François Le Diascorn
THE SHEPHERD,
MONT-SAINT-MICHEL, FRANCE

Ten years ago, on a trip to Honduras, I visited camps housing Salvadoran refugees. During my visit, death squads from El Salvador crossed the border, entered one of the camps and abducted about 40 men, carrying them off, attached by their thumbs. Though our delegation was armed only with cameras, we decided to follow them along a riverbed, accompanied by the refugees' mothers, wives and children. As we got closer to the death squads, the question of whether they were going to kill us became more and more real.

Finally they were within earshot, and they realized we might catch up with them. We said to them: "If you kill us, people will know. You can't kill everybody." And for some strange reason, they set the refugees free. It was like a dream to be alive after believing we were going to die. That day I saw how important it is to help save a human life. It was a turning point in my life to have been right there as people I perceived as innocent were almost killed before my eyes. It helped me see that for some, life simply means survival. In El Salvador life is a question of justice: the right to have children, the right to live without fear of malnutrition, torture or murder. It helped me see that for my life to have purpose, I must come to terms with what is just and what is unjust.

Bianca Jagger
is an actress and filmmaker working on a documentary about her native Nicaragua

A thin red thread, from the heart, under the clothes, reaches the white hand, trickling among the rings. The fragile woman's body, supine on the armchair, no longer utters breath or thought.

On the sunny streets of Palermo, the assassins walk. Under the well-tailored jacket you don't notice the swelling of the weapon. And so it happens that, with a smile, you say, "Good day," and lose, yet again, the chance to ask them the meaning of life.

The assassins take a walk as the skies become blacker, as breath becomes shorter and species disappear. They walk as a surprise bomb annihilates the just-born wonder of the adolescent.

Letizia Battaglia,
Italian photographer and theater director, is a deputy in the Sicilian parliament

Life is something you measure not in years but in precious moments— and in how you value those moments. The responsibility for making such moments meaningful is yours alone. There are no definitions of failure or success except the ones you specify for yourself. You are the meaning of your own life.

I believe, however, that self-indulgent goals lead nowhere in this world or the next. I believe you are living life to its utmost when you are actively involved in making a change to better the whole community. When you are engaged in the lives of others, you become a dynamic example of humanity's vital spirit. I see my life in this collective sense. Whatever I can achieve in this life, whatever I can stand up for—that is what my children and yours will inherit. You and I, as living beings, are portals connecting the past and future.

For my part, I have chosen to try to live nonviolently. I cannot do harm to others. By living this way, I encourage others to do the same, to choose happiness and not sadness.

Mubarak Awad
is the Palestinian-born director of Non-Violence International

In 1945 my father's life was beautiful. The goodies had won, the baddies had lost, and truth had prevailed. For some years he was a very good Communist Party member. He served on the Central Committee. But he was a man of extreme conscience. In his last 20 years he felt guilty for everything that had happened in the name of the party. He was one of the first to complain in the '50s and '60s, one of the first to lose his job. He eventually joined Charter 77, a human rights group. He died of a heart attack after three interrogations with the state security police. The strongest, most meaningful moment in my life was my father's death. It made me realize the importance of conscience. He always told me: "Never exchange your conscience for the belief that some party or someone else knows better." He paid the price for his belief—the ultimate price.

I have benefited from this. We have won as Communism has fallen; I can feel pride in having helped a tiny bit. But I can also say that I have survived by not making compromises. My conscience is clear. For me, political resistance was a question of survival, of being able to face myself. I remember a very important moment in my teens when I heard Bob Dylan singing, "When you ain't got nothing, you got nothing to lose." There was a time when I was afraid of losing. Now I know I can have five cars one day and no cars the next and it won't do anything to me as a person. I would like to die in my boots, being on my own, being able to give to others, not having compromised.

Jan Urban,
journalist for a Prague daily newspaper, was a leading member of Charter 77, a dissident human rights organization under the former Communist regime

I believe in fate. I think that the meaning of life is to make your life coincide with your fate. If you watch carefully, you can see certain coincidences or patterns that recur and indicate what you are supposed to do in life. If there had not been political changes in my country, I would never have become world champion. When I understood it was the right time, I felt I had to fill this role, not only as world champion but also as a figure embodying perestroika and my nation's new emphasis on individual rights. O.K., I was lucky. But I was able to accomplish what others could not: to matter as an individual.

The first time I addressed a mass demonstration in Moscow I was speechless for the first 10 seconds. I was standing on a platform in the middle of a sea of people, to the left, to the right, behind me. And at that moment I understood the determination of the people to change their lives. I felt so proud and amazed. I was completely fulfilled. I was witnessing humanity's greatest accomplishment: a group of people changing the historical process that could have dominated them forever. It made me feel that maybe my reason for being was to be part of this revolution, to symbolize the possibilities that exist for my people. For one of the first times in modern Soviet history, an individual could *be* the system yet at the same time could *represent* the oppressed, those fighting an inhuman regime. This gave people hope.

We cannot play with our destinies. As in chess, if you have a chance in life, you cannot tease it. You must go for it.

Gary Kasparov,
Soviet chess Grandmaster from Azerbaijan, has held the title of World Chess Champion since 1985

A scroll of superb calligraphy by the great 19th century Chinese translator Yen Fu enjoys a special place in my living room. It contains a poem in the classical style, composed by Yen himself and dedicated to my grandfather. Probably because of its erudite literary references and the flowing style of the brushwork, it escaped the censure of the Red Guard and survived the Cultural Revolution. Actually, the poem's sentiments are rather bitter. Looking back on his legacy as the man who introduced Adam Smith, Montesquieu and others to the Chinese people, he cast doubt on these efforts, calling his life's work "utterly futile."

I have tried, in a more modest way, to accomplish similar goals. Not by expounding on the wealth of nations or the origin of species, but by working in a more frivolous arena—the stage and screen. All the same, the scroll of venerable Mr. Yen serves as a constant reminder. Will I one day lament my wasted efforts in having tried to present and stage Shakespeare, Arthur Miller and others to a Chinese audience?

Somehow I don't think so. One advantage of living in the 20th century is the access to feedback, pleasant and otherwise. Mr. Yen Fu, through no fault of his own, had no idea of the lasting impact of his work and, if we take into account what the intelligentsia have had to go through, could not be blamed for his bitterness. I have been luckier. My faith in the ultimate solidarity of the human race and the inherent congenial emotions of mankind has been confirmed, time and again, by the laughter and tears of audiences worldwide and in my homeland.

Mr. Yen's scroll, however, remains a reminder. To bridge gaps between nations takes much more than one man, or one generation.

Ying Ruocheng,
China's former Vice Minister of Culture, is a renowned actor and director

When you ask me about the meaning of life, I remember a Mister Softee ice cream van.

The summer after the coup that ousted my father, who had been the Prime Minister of Ghana, I was visiting Philadelphia. One day, while running for a bus, I heard the sound of a Mister Softee van. It stopped me in my tracks. I bought the ice cream and found myself crying, standing in the middle of the street.

Until then, I had not faced the reality of the coup, the memory of the sound of gun battles that had raged outside our house, the fact that I was exiled from home a second time. I suddenly realized that I had survived the bullets and that I was actually alive to do something as ordinary and trivial as eating ice cream. This was a moment to treasure. Life can be that simple, that joyful. I made a commitment that day to treasure life, no matter what it brought.

Abena Busia,
exiled Ghanaian poet, lives in New York City

F ellow from LIFE calls up wanting me to tell him "the meaning of life" for a survey he's conducting. He'd written me about it. "I haven't been able to write anything," I tell him.

"Perhaps," he says, "you could tell me on the phone."

"The phone's probably tapped," I tell him, "and I'd get in deep trouble telling Everything, spilling the beans, so to speak, like a mole in the inner office."

"I'd keep it a secret," he tells me, with a question mark in his voice.

"But that's just it," I tell him. "That's why nobody can tell you the Meaning. It's a secret."

Lawrence Ferlinghetti,
Beat Generation poet, painter and translator, wrote *A Coney Island of the Mind*

Volker Hinz
DINER, ORLANDO

Actually, I do know the meaning of life. But I see no reason to share it. Have a nice millennium.

Gore Vidal
is an American novelist, essayist and screenwriter

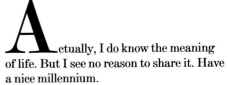

Theo Westenberger
ROCK STAR DAVID LEE ROTH'S ROOM,
WESTIN HOTEL, DETROIT

Arthur Tress
SNOWBOUND STILL LIFE,
YOSEMITE NATIONAL PARK

Linda Connor
ENTWINED BUDDHA,
AYUTHAYA, THAILAND

All life comes from the Panchamama. Without her there is nothing—no harvest, no fire, no seasons, no dreams. Without Panchamama we would not even have a place to be. I serve the Panchamama, and she gives me knowledge to help people in her honor. It is the power of Panchamama that lets me cure the sick or see the evil feeding on a person's mind. When you are hungry or thirsty or tired, so is the Panchamama. Serve her first, before yourself, as you would an elder or an infant or a guest.

We live a certain time until our death arrives, and then we turn to stone, water or star. If you led a bad life, you'll wind up as water, which never rests and changes form. If your life was normal, you will become stone, solid and without pain. And if your life was exemplary, you become a star in the sky so everyone can see your light.

We live in the Panchamama herself. Whatever we need—food and drink, the animals and birds, the soil and sky, the rivers and mountains—belong to her.

Panchamama gives us life, but we must pay her price. For a good life, pay Panchamama before you take her favors. Once a need is met people tend to forget about it. But if you take without paying, you're a thief and you'll be punished.

We either work or we die. We must work to eat and to pay the Panchamama.

Ema Rivas
is a priestess of the Panchamama in La Paz, Bolivia

201

I want to tell you something. I'm 93, and I really like to be my age. That's what makes my life meaningful now. Everybody wants to know how old I am. I don't know why, but they do. It really tickles me. A while back I had to have some cataracts removed. Then I got to where I couldn't walk. I was just too doggone old to get around. Then I got sick. They said I had acute bronchitis and an infected kidney and I don't know what else. I wasn't worth killing I was so weak and worn out and tired and ornery. I couldn't even walk out to pick up my newspaper at the bottom of the hill in the morning. I'd have told you life wasn't worth living.

What's kept me going is that there are so many interesting things going on in the world and I just want to know what's going to happen next. There's a lot of things going on in the federal government that I think's asinine. The thing that kept me interested in living after I was sick was when all those banks went kaflooey and the government had to pick up the tab for all those billions of dollars. I just want to know what's going to happen with that. I have natural curiosity about things. That keeps me going. My main reason for living right now may be so I can bellyache and fuss and cuss. To me, what life is is living long enough to see how things come out. I'm afraid I'll miss something if I die.

Ellen Spendrup,

former postal employee, U.S. Army office worker and secretary-treasurer of the Neshoba, Mississippi, county fair, has raised mink and silver fox in Sweden

Kurt Smith
BIRTHDAY PARTY

We are in the world like one classroom of elementary school children, together according to age, let out onto the playground for recess, unsupervised. There are the children who play easily together in a circle, the girl who sits alone in the corner, the boy whom other children chase and throw stones at, the few good students, walking with their hands in their pockets, figuring out problems, the dreamers, writing with sticks in the sand, the noisy crowd and the silent hurt one hugging his hurt knee. There are those who torment and disturb and frighten others who are weaker or different, through no cause of their own. There are those who exploit and those who are kind. The balance seems always to remain the same, and so the world goes on. All my life, I seem to meet the same children I knew on my first grade playground, only with different faces and new names. Perhaps our journey in life is to recognize our own part in the pageant, to see ourselves as the bullies or the saints or the revelers or tormentors or the dreamers we are, and to work for the days of our lives to adjust that position only a little bit toward the good.

Mona Simpson,
American novelist and short-story writer,
is the author of *Anywhere But Here*

John Dominis
DORI, PAUL AND AH CHOU
AT PLAY, HONG KONG

(Overleaf)
Sam Abell
KENTUCKY SHAKER TOWN
AT PLEASANT HILL

Life is a conscious space between two eternities. It is a canyon separating never from forever. It is the realm where feelings are born in both spirit and flesh. Life only gives meaning to the time a man lives. Only the living have meaning.

That's why all men—and cultures and countries—should leave a work reflecting what they found in life. It's our task to master the medium or instrument which will express our internal life in external form. For a writer, a pen; for a musician, a song; for a farmer, a tree; for an engineer, a bridge; for a teacher, a school. The projection of man in his work is the meaning of life. Unless a man creates something outside himself, the meaning of his life will vanish at the instant of his death.

Each man is the artist of his life, and each life is a portrait of the man. You are either a man or a moocher, and there is nothing in between. The decision is entirely yours. Humans have to choose to be people. That's what separates us from animals.

Domingo Moles

is a musician and tango composer from Buenos Aires, Argentina

The meaning of life is to be found in our surroundings and in our relationships—our relationships with one another, with our natural and industrial environments, with technologies shaping our present and future.

Life is meaningful when we respect the best of tradition while still loving innovation, when we care about our families while not ignoring the extended families with whom we share our communities, when we invest our material, spiritual and human resources wisely.

Life is fulfilling when we marry pride with tolerance, when our deeds and our words are nourished by hope and by realism, when the wisdom of the ages catches the passionate eye of youth.

Life on this earth in our time is, above all, a parade of interdependent peoples, interdependent ideas, interdependent solutions. We are all artists of the possible—and dreamers of that which is just now beyond our reach, but may not be tomorrow.

Youssou N'Dour

is a Senegalese singer and the leader of the West African dance band Super Etoile de Dakar

It is quite clear that we cannot *know* why we are here. But it is permissible (indeed necessary) to attempt to search out from all resources available to us (including our imagination, intelligence, memory and history) the conditions that may enhance our sojourn.

I take my bearing from a peculiar creation story of my people, the Igbo of southeastern Nigeria. The crux of this story is that Chukwu, the Creator, saw the primordial Igbo kings of Nri and Adama sitting disconsolate on an anthill one morning and asked them what the matter was. From their conversation we learn that humans were still wandering like wild animals in the bush. "What about the yam I gave you to plant?" asked God. "The soil is too wet," replied the kings. God then directed them to go to the town of blacksmiths, Awka, to ask a blacksmith to blow the soil dry with his bellows.

The point of the story, I take it, is that creation is a continuing process; that the world was never "finished" and found to be good, as in the book of Genesis. It is only potentially good and requires consultation between the Creator and humankind to make it habitable.

One meaning of our life, then, is the opportunity and challenge it presents to us for participation in the continuous process of creation—through discussion and cooperative work rather than conflict.

Chinua Achebe,

Nigerian author, is one of Africa's most acclaimed novelists

Nobody really knows why we're here, obviously. There are big pieces missing from the pictures offered us by science and religion. Based on our present knowledge, the whole thing simply doesn't make sense. But what's so wonderful is that we want it to make sense, and our need for meaning drives us relentlessly to create. Cave paintings, totem poles, villages, cathedrals—it is a never-ending process. Sometimes I think we have become the creative gods and goddesses of our myths and dreams.

How absolutely astonishing that we bring to a universe of green grass and blue skies the wholly new phenomenon of a violin concerto, a hologram, a ballerina on point.

If we do have a purpose, maybe it is to join with the evolutionary process through our complex artistic creation. Our stories and poems and lasers are as significant as diamonds or gold or angelfish.

And of course, in the very midst of all this, we strive to be good. We believe in being good. We never give up on it. Eden isn't only a memory, it's a promise, because we are better than the lion and the lamb; we understand them as symbols; we can make the world a wholesome garden. And no other being under the sun has ever been able to conceive of such a thing.

I don't know why we're here. But there is so much to be done! How simply wonderful to be alive.

Anne Rice,

Gothic novelist, is the author of the Vampire Chronicles trilogy

The history of humanity has never had a chapter devoid of conflict, turbulence, violence. What humanity has needed most of all down through the ages has been serenity of mind. And in this I have found the reason for my existence. In my own way, I do my best to help people achieve serenity of mind by practicing one of our strictly traditional cults: tea ceremonies. I lacquer utensils—lovingly and painstakingly crafted tea trays, dippers, whisks and caddies—required in observing that cult. For 400 years members of my family have taken turns dedicating themselves to this trade.

In a small tatamied room, guests and hosts alike sit quietly, going through prescribed routines for serving or enjoying bowls of green tea. That cult is known as *sado,* the way of tea. That, as far as I'm concerned, is the finest way to attain spiritual serenity, a state of mind that is vital if one is to have a happy existence.

Sotetsu Nakamura,

of Kyoto, is a 12th generation master lacquerer of utensils used in Japanese tea ceremonies and the first woman to head her ancestral atelier

Inge Morath
STILL LIFE, NEAR
KOSTROMA, ROSSIYSKAYA

All of us struggle toward commitments or involvements that extend beyond our immediate relationships and our limited lifespan. Elderly people reminisce and contemplate what their lives have meant in order to assure themselves that their lives have had significance and that some of their acts will reverberate into the future.

Humans can be distinguished by three attributes: We know that we die, we live in culture, and we are symbolizers, re-creating everything we experience. There is no special philosophical or ethical reason for our being here. We are not here for any greater purpose than the rest of nature is, but we do have this marvelous capacity to construct meanings, to construct our own sense of purpose. One of the main concepts we tend to share is that of being involved with human history and with the perpetuation of certain ideas, influences and beliefs.

For people of all cultures, the meaning of life is bound up with what I call the symbolization of immortality—the sense we require of living on in our children and their children, a larger spiritual or religious principle in our influences on other human beings, or what is widely symbolized as "eternal nature." This expression of larger human connectedness is neither rational nor irrational, is consistent with reason, broadly defined, and is a powerful aspect of human existence.

Robert Jay Lifton,
psychiatrist and psychohistorian, is the author
of *Death in Life: Survivors of Hiroshima*

Chuck O'Rear
NOON PRAYERS,
ISTIQLAL MOSQUE, JAKARTA

Bruno Barbey
EASTER WEEK PILGRIMS, POLAND

(Overleaf)
Lynn Hyman Butler
MERRY-GO-ROUND, CONEY ISLAND

Contributors

A

146
Kareem
Abdul-Jabbar

76
Salma Abu-Quaoud

209
Chinua Achebe

50
Laurie Anderson

142
Corazon Aquino

185
Jeffrey Archer

113
Freddy Arévalo

146
Arthur Ashe

B

196
Mubarak Awad

122
Francis Bacon

162
Amiri Baraka

87
Adolfo Barcella

96
Lynda Barry

119
Gert Bastian

149
Mary Catherine
Bateson

196
Letizia Battaglia

17
I Dewa Nyoman
Batuan

118
Menachem Begin

164
Philip Berg

107
Yogi Berra

25
Guru
Bhagwandasacharya

118
Benazir Bhutto

153
Harold Bloom

61
Charles Bloomhall

132
Rok Boleslav

C

159
Rabiap Boonma

103
Panchi Bor

51
Billy Bragg

162
Gwendolyn Brooks

197
Abena Busia

76
Giles Carlyle-Clarke

52
Henri
Cartier-Bresson

169
Carlos Carvalo

90
Joseph Chaikin

50
Ray Charles

177
Cicciolina

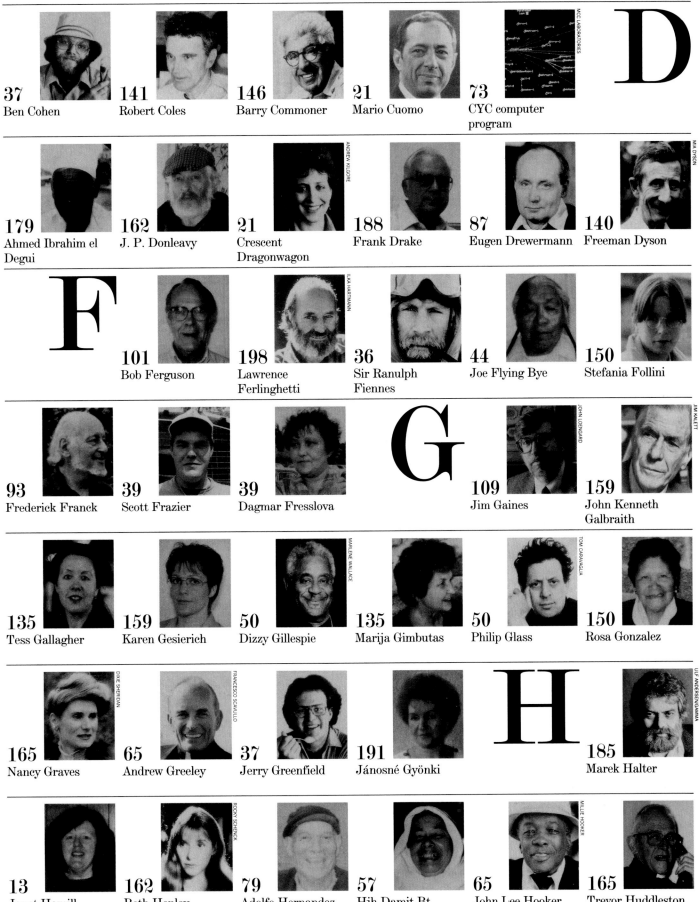

D

37 Ben Cohen

141 Robert Coles

146 Barry Commoner

21 Mario Cuomo

73 CYC computer program

179 Ahmed Ibrahim el Degui

162 J. P. Donleavy

21 Crescent Dragonwagon

188 Frank Drake

87 Eugen Drewermann

140 Freeman Dyson

F

101 Bob Ferguson

198 Lawrence Ferlinghetti

36 Sir Ranulph Fiennes

44 Joe Flying Bye

150 Stefania Follini

93 Frederick Franck

39 Scott Frazier

39 Dagmar Fresslova

G

109 Jim Gaines

159 John Kenneth Galbraith

135 Tess Gallagher

159 Karen Gesierich

50 Dizzy Gillespie

135 Marija Gimbutas

50 Philip Glass

150 Rosa Gonzalez

H

165 Nancy Graves

65 Andrew Greeley

37 Jerry Greenfield

191 Jánosné Gyönki

185 Marek Halter

13 Janet Hamill

162 Beth Henley

79 Adolfo Hernandez

57 Hjh Damit Bt Hjpiut

65 John Lee Hooker

165 Trevor Huddleston

I

90
Abdullah Ibrahim

103
Mustafa Ibrahim

65
Ice-T

J

27
Michael Jackson

196
Bianca Jagger

169
Raja Nor Jasmin

33
Angelo Jaspe

122
Bill T. Jones

192
Charlotte Jones

114
Albert Joyce

K

69
Anne Kamande

47
László Kardos

197
Gary Kasparov

68
Yoshitake Kawamoto

44
Garrison Keillor

187
Salif Keita

119
Petra Kelly

163
Yashar Kemal

95
Margarita Kenetic

31
Jeffry Keroh

122
Jack Kevorkian

169
Vicky Khano

105
Joel Kinagwi

51
B. B. King

20
Marwa Kisare

181
Marek Kotanski

51
KRS-ONE

93
Barbara Kruger

132
Günter Kunert

L

17
Jaron Lanier

44
Queen Latifah

175
Norman Lear

31
Arturo Leguía

136
Elmore Leonard

80
David Letterman

212
Robert Jay Lifton

NOT PICTURED
87
Ding Lili

NOT PICTURED
31
Chief Linchwe II

189
Fang Lizhi

132
Glenn Lockhart

65
Sophia Loren

188
Sir Bernard Lovell

31
James Lovelock

103
Mercedes Loyola

132
Earl Lu

156
José Antonio
Lutzenberger

M

146
Elle Macpherson

163
Naguib Mahfouz

91
Mustapha
Mahmoud

44
Emran Md Majid

91
Raymundo Marca

145
Marcel Marceau

113
Wynton Marsalis

24
Yehudi Menuhin

178
Concepción
Méndez

61
Michael Metzen

76
Lailene Middleton

167
Midori

80
Spike Milligan

209
Domingo Moles

147
Luc Montagnier

57
Padee Moothoo

169
Mike Morris

97
Thomas Morris

95
Jabulani Moyo

65
V. Y. Mudimbe

147
Jemimah Mwakisha

N

NOT
PICTURED

182
Monk N

211
Sotetsu Nakamura

10
Gloria Naylor

209
Youssou N'Dour

78
Rupert Neudeck

171
Ingrid Newkirk

124
Valeria Nunns

O

17
Sinéad O'Connor

68
Mira Odi

61
Teresa O'Dwyer

57 Juliana Omale

51 Yoko Ono

91 Ayano Otani

P

31 Kudang Ak Panyu

NOT PICTURED
95 Loy Parass

91 Tatjana Patitz

144 Milorad Pavić

191 Fanniedell Peeples

119 Claiborne Pell

80 Sean Penn

84 Roger Tory Peterson

150 Philippe Petit

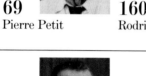
69 Pierre Petit

160 Rodrigo Poblette

76 Zdenka Podrouzkova

191 Alvin Poussaint

105 Nelda Jo Powell

115 Sergei Prikhodko

39 J. B. Pursley

R

76 Sue Ellen Radovich

90 Kanda Anuman Rajadhon

146 Mary Lou Retton

209 Anne Rice

163 Jeremy Rifkin

201 Ema Rivas

103 Cesar Rodriguez

20 Oscar Rodriguez

197 Ying Ruocheng

S

153 Muhammad Ruslan bin Abdullah

142 Nawal el Saadawi

90 Felipe Sagardia

137 Jonas Salk

70 Barry Sanders

NOT PICTURED
103 Angelina Santamaria

191 Aye Saung

153 Nabil Sawalha

130 Dave Scott

135 Richard Serra

41 Cory SerVaas

113 V. S. Seturaman

142 Natan Sharansky

119 Eduard Shevardnadze

90 Bernie Siegel

204 Mona Simpson

169 Beverly Ann Smith

54 Jessica Smith

54 Patti Smith

54 Sylvestre Sorola

203 Ellen Spendrup

39 Miklós Szabo

T

40 Betty Teska

95 Ilir Tivari

61 Terry Tracy

121 Cokorda Tstri Ratih Tryani

122 Abraham Twerski

U

196 Jan Urban

V

80 Melvin Van Peebles

185 Miklós Vásárhelyi

118 Simone Veil

199 Gore Vidal

W

185 Dorothy Walpole

65 William Warrior

135 Lina Wertmuller

69 Elie Wiesel

68 Simon Wiesenthal

18 Robert Wilkoske

54 Marianne Williamson

105 Oprah Winfrey

109 Steven Wright

X

53 Yang Xianyi

Y

84 Wang Yani

49 Maharishi Mahesh Yogi

Z

105 Franco Zeffirelli

Photographers

Abell, Sam 206
Adams, Shelby Lee 58
Adelman, Bob 96
Allard, William Albert 77
Anonymous 114
Atwood, Jane Evelyn 53
Azel, José 41

Balog, James 134
Barbey, Bruno 213
Barrat, Martine 98
Beernink, Gerlo 47
Benson, Harry 126
Berry, Ian 71
Brack, Dennis 193
Bryson, John 100
Burri, René 124
Burt, Brad 15
Butler, Lynn Hyman 214

Cartier-Bresson, Henri 86
Cernan, Eugene A./NASA 188
Chadwick, Helen 172
Chesley, Paul 48
Clarkson, Rich 131
Cobb, Jodi 63
Connor, Linda 201
Courtney-Clarke, Margaret 56
Cruz, Marco A. 22

De Giulio, Robert 158
DeVore III, Nicholas 60
Dominis, John 204

Earth Satellite Corporation 72
Eppridge, Bill 89

Farber, Don 223
Ferorelli, Enrico 108
Ferrato, Donna 42
Fischer, Georg 40

Fisher, Angela 106
Fitzhugh, Susie 167
Foley, Bill 166
Franck, Martine 29
Frare, Therese 180
Friedel, Michael 156

Galligani, Mauro 32
García Rodero, Cristina 151
Ginn, Victoria 30
Ginsberg, Allen 133
Goldin, Nan 97
Goldsmith, Lynn 64
Gottfried, Arlene 187
Greenberg, Mark 165
Grinker, Lori 88
Guichard, Jean 10

Halstead, Dirck 120
Hayflick, Leonard 24
Heiden, David 94
Henriette, Catherine 6
Herold, Werner 34
Heyman, Abigail 178
Heyman, Ken 82
Higgins, Dan 109
Hinz, Volker 198
Hiser, David 83
Hockney, David 92
Horan, Kevin 81
Hosoe, Eikoh 173
Hudson, Derek 78

Iwago, Mitsuaki 152

Jarecke, Kenneth 115
Johnson, Dion 28
Johnson, Lynn 55

Kelsh, Nick 190
Kennerly, David Hume 183
Krivtsov, Pavel 46
Kubota, Hiroji 164
Kunkel, Dennis 25

Lanker, Brian 26
Lanting, Frans 112
Lecuona, Antoine 160
Le Diascorn, François 194
Leibovitz, Annie 179
Leifer, Neil 143

Lessing, Erich 208
Loengard, John 168

Magubane, Peter 129
Maisel, Jay 205
Malin, David 148
Malloch, Roger 144
Masats, Ramón 174
Mason, Charles 170
McCurry, Steve 104
McNally, Joe 8
Means, Kaia 154
Melford, Michael 101
Morath, Inge 210
Morris, Christopher 14
Moyer, Robin 184
Muscionico, Tomas 107

Naito, Masatoshi 186
Newton, Helmut 74
Nilsson, Lennart 149
Nixon, Nicholas 110

O'Brien, Michael 128
O'Rear, Chuck 212

Parker, David 155
Pavlovsky, Jacques 161
Pinkhassov, Georgi 16
Plachy, Sylvia 75

Regan, Ken 62
Rentmeester, Co 123
Riboud, Marc 140
Richards, Eugene 116
Robert, Patrick 79
Rošický, Petr 138
Rossi, Joe 52
Rubin, Steven 70

Sacha, Bob 137
Saga, Teiji 84
Salgado, Sebastião 38
Saul, April 136
Schermeister, Phil 45
Schmitz, Walter 37
Sennet, Mark 141
Sichov, Vladimir 125
Slavin, Neal 102
Smith, Kurt 202
Suau, Anthony 145

Teufel, Heinz 176
Thoma, Michael 130
Tress, Arthur 200
Tuttle, Merlin D. 18

Uchiyama, Sumio 12
Ullal, Jay 7, 66

Webb, Alex 36
Wells, David H. 182
Westenberger, Theo 199
Wilson, Wes 192

Yurchenko, Marina 121

PICTURE SOURCES

Agence Vu 151
Anglo Australian Observatory 148
Bat Conservation International 18
Bilderberg 37, 40
Black Star 14, 55, 134, 145, 170, 193
Bonnier Fakta 149
Camera 5 62
Contact Press Images 41, 53, 88, 107, 115, 179
Earth Satellite Corporation, GEOPIC® 72
Robert Estall Photographs 106
Gamma-Liaison 120, 183, 199
GLMR Associés 10
©David Hockney 1983 92
IMAGENLATINA 22
JB Pictures 70, 182
LGI 64
Magnum Photos 16, 29, 36, 38, 71, 86, 104, 116, 124, 140, 144, 164, 208, 210, 213
Minden Pictures 112
©National Geographic Society 63, 77
NFK Photo Agency 47
Ottawa (KS) Herald 192
The Philadelphia Inquirer 136
Photo Researchers 84
Photographers/Aspen 45, 48, 60, 83
Rapho 194
Rockford (IL) Register Star 15
Seattle Post-Intelligencer 158
Shooting Back 28
Sipa Press 125
St. Paul (MN) Pioneer Press 52
Stern 7, 66, 198
Sygma 78, 79, 114, 160, 161
Visions 165
West Light 212

page 12: courtesy Thames and Hudson
page 110: courtesy Zabriskie Gallery
page 172: photograph made with Mark Pilkington
page 173: courtesy Howard Greenberg Gallery

Don Farber
BROTHERS AT A TIBETAN BUDDHIST
MONASTERY, DARJEELING, INDIA